More Advance Praise for *Who's Your Gladys?*

"Many companies think they deliver great customer service. This book will remind you that there is a lot to learn. It is filled with great company examples and strategies you can use immediately. Start reading this and begin a new journey on creating world class customer service!"—**Lisa Ford, business speaker on customer issues; author, *Exceptional Customer Service***

"*Who's Your Gladys?* is a powerful and inspiring guide for creating enviable customer service and lasting relationships with your customers and staff." —**Stephanie Wolf, CEO, SportsMind**

"We have all had 'Gladyses' in our lives, and too often we get hooked and react in a less than positive way. In their book, Marilyn Suttle and Lori Jo Vest have given us real-life stories and specific action ideas to see both our internal and external Gladyses as unique human beings, not just as inconveniences to be tolerated. This is a thought-provoking 'how-to' book about creating extraordinary, caring customer *experiences* wherever your workplace may be!"—**Barbara Glanz, author, *The Simple Truths of Service Inspired by Johnny the Bagger®*, *CARE Packages for Your Customers*, and *CARE Packages for the Workplace***

"In their new book, Marilyn Suttle and Lori Jo Vest examine the complexities of the relationship between corporations and consumers. By offering examples of stumbling blocks and solutions, they break down the barriers between the two sides and offer practical, humanistic, and attainable ways to make the relationships win-win. This is an invaluable how-to book for anyone looking to incorporate successful human interaction into complex business relationships." —**Raz Ingrasci, President and CEO, Hoffman Institute Foundation**

"Powerful and practical tips on creating exemplary customer service in your own organization."—**Randy Gage, author, *Prosperity Mind***

"If you are not reading and applying Suttle and Vest's book on how to capture and keep the best customers, you are not growing your business. It is as simple as that!"—**Thomas J. Winninger, America's Business Makeover Specialist, bestselling author, and President, Winninger Family Companies**

"Quality customer service defines high-performing organizations, and with this book, Suttle and Vest take us inside some of the best examples of meeting and exceeding customer needs. Fun, highly readable and applicable to every business that desires to serve its customers and grow."—**Keith A. Pretty, J.D., President and CEO, Northwood University**

"A great story, a great lesson, a great book!"—**Greg Godek, author, *1001 Ways to Be Romantic***

Who's Your Gladys?

How to Turn Even the
Most Difficult Customer Into
Your Biggest Fan

MARILYN SUTTLE and
LORI JO VEST

⁄AMACOM

American Management Association

New York • Atlanta • Brussels • Chicago • Mexico City • San Francisco
Shanghai • Tokyo • Toronto • Washington, D.C.

Special discounts on bulk quantities of AMACOM books are available to corporations, professional associations, and other organizations. For details, contact Special Sales Department, AMACOM, a division of American Management Association, 1601 Broadway, New York, NY 10019.
Tel.: 800-250-5308 Fax: 518-891-2372
E-mail: specialsls@amanet.org
Website: www.amacombooks.org/go/specialsales
To view all AMACOM titles go to: www.amacombooks.org

This publication is designed to provide accurate and authoritative information in regard to the subject matter covered. It is sold with the understanding that the publisher is not engaged in rendering legal, accounting, or other professional service. If legal advice or other expert assistance is required, the services of a competent professional person should be sought.

Library of Congress Cataloging-in-Publication Data

Suttle, Marilyn.
    Who's your Gladys? : how to turn even the most difficult customer into your biggest fan / Marilyn Suttle and Lori Jo Vest.
        p.   cm.
    Includes bibliographical references and index.
    ISBN-13: 978-0-8144-1439-2
    ISBN-10: 0-8144-1439-7
    1. Customer services.   2. Customer relations.   3. Interpersonal relations.   4. Customer services—Case studies.   5. Customer relations—Case studies. I. Vest, Lori Jo.   II. Title.
    HF5415.5.S885   2009
    658.8'12—dc22
                                                                                            2009013269

Printing number

10   9   8   7   6   5   4   3   2   1

Contents

Foreword

Today, if someone took a poll of your customers and asked if you matter to them, how do you think you would come out? If as a business you ceased to exist tomorrow, do you think anyone would really care? In other words, has your product, service, or brand established an emotional connection with your customers to the extent that they are invested in your enduring success?

This is the deep soul-searching question I want you to ask yourself. Does your company matter to your customers? Really, honestly, answer this. Are you a positive force in their lives? If you disappeared, would their lives be diminished in some way? I think if you tell yourself the truth, you might even conclude, "Well, not so much." Will we shed any tears if Tide laundry detergent is not on the shelves anymore? No, probably not. Will we shed some tears if Southwest Airlines suddenly ceased to exist? We might. And if Apple ceased to exist? Yeah, probably.

Do you, in fact, matter? You know you want the answer to be yes. But would it be?

If you're an entrepreneur, a product manager, or a CEO reading this, ask yourself, "Do we really matter to our customers?" If you are honest with yourself, you might say, "Here's where maybe we matter, and here's where maybe we don't." Are you connecting with customers on an emotional level? Are you even seeing the whole picture and getting accurate feedback on the customer experience without irritating them during the survey process? Do your customers care if you live or die? You definitely want that answer to be "Yes."

This book will live in the customer service category on search engines. The two words are so overused that you can easily miss the real meaning of the term. First off, what you think represents great service may not in fact be what matters to your customers. This book will show you how to get clear about what actually does. As you read the stories and focus on the principles revealed, consider that you are actually in the customer *experience* business and that your product or service is really a delivery vehicle for providing your customers with a great experience that matters to them.

There are a lot of books out there about customer service. I just did an Amazon Books search using the two words "customer service" and got a return of 81,313 occurrences! So why would you buy this book? Because the authors have done a terrific job of telling enlightening stories of exemplary customer service and the lessons to be learned from each engaging story. Most importantly they show you how to specifically apply each of these principles in your daily business life (a lot of them will work with your spouse as well). They provide you with a system to measure and track your progress. This last piece is essential. You cannot improve without measurement. The book is worth the time for this alone.

Read this book and put the principles to work. Do this and you will be able to become a CEO—we're talking *Chief Experience Officer*. Then you'll be able to change your company and your life for the better and make a difference that matters in the lives of others—really!

Stewart Emery, bestselling coauthor of *Success Built to Last* and *Do You Matter?*

Acknowledgments

From Marilyn

To my talented writing partner, Lori, who made this process such a joyful adventure. Your wisdom and compassion contribute so much to this planet, and I am so glad that I get to call you my friend.

To my supportive husband, Cliff, and my wise beyond their years sons, Lance and Alex, whom I love so much. I am a better person for having you in my life.

To my dear mother, Rose, my encouraging brother and sister-in-law, Chris and Hannah, my inspiring sister and brother-in-law, Linda and Dave, you bring such value and fun into my life. To my family members who have passed: my dad, Andrew, and my sister Nancy, whose kind hearts stay with me always, and all my extended family members, you are a blessing.

To my mentor Jack Canfield, who taught me to transform my dreams into reality and make a quantum leap into professional success with love and joy. And to the Canfield Companies' fabulous employees, and assisting staff, with big hugs for Patty Aubery, Robert MacPhee, and Jesse Ianniello.

To my friends, colleagues, and role models who offered sage advice along the way: Marci Shimoff, Lynn Robinson, Rebecca Morgan, and Holly Stiel, and all my fabulous National Speakers Association friends.

To my professional coach, Jo Erickson, whose expertise in NLP and family constellation has given me greater access to my creativity and inner resources.

To my Monday Morning Visions group: Jana Stanfield, who was an endless source of referrals, Lenora Boyle, Deb Sandella, Dianne Legro, Betsy Wiersma, and Jan Black, all talented, lovely women who inspire me beyond belief.

To Adele Faber and Elaine Mazlish, for their transformational parenting books and the kind support they gave me when I facilitated their programs: You had a profound effect on the way I learned to communicate and teach.

To my BFFs: Annamarie Pitt, Shari Sonnenberg, and Diane Tsaprasis.

From Lori

To my expert relationship guru and writing partner, Marilyn, whose enthusiasm, patience, and overall genius contributed so greatly and made the process of creating this book so much fun. I never could have done this without you, girlfriend. (And I wouldn't have wanted to!)

To my sweet husband, Ron Wingard, who gave me the time, support, and tools (a MacBook!) to complete this book project during early morning, weekend, and late night writing sessions while I still worked full-time at my day job. His never-ending love and patience, in spite of my overwrought schedule and bossy personality, are amazing.

To my son, Kyle Ellsasser, whose commitment to being nice to other people is so inspiring. At 10 years old, he already gets what's truly important in life.

To Jeff Carter, the owner of Communicore Visual Communications, for letting me try so many of the practices we learned on this project at his company, and for his constant support of just about anything new that I want to try, both professionally and personally.

To my boss at my first "real job," David E. Laster, who taught me so much of what I know about how to take care of customers. His guidance early in my career made an incredible difference in who I am in business.

To my friend and coworker Candice Lazar, whose belief in and support of anything we tried at Communicore helped make it a success. She's one of the smartest and most engaged people I know. Can't wait to see where her career takes her.

To my boss at my first production industry job, Gary May, for telling me over and over, "Don't bring me problems, bring me solutions!" His commitment to mentoring and training young people in the production business is legendary.

To the clients and staff at Communicore, who put up with me and support a caring and compassionate way of doing business. This extraordinary group of people makes it a pleasure to go to work every day. Because of you, Communicore is a great place where much laughter rings through the halls.

To M. K. Seipke, whose early enthusiasm and wise advice inspired me to make this book happen. It's amazing how one person can make such a difference over lunch.

From Both of Us

To all the amazing company leaders and employees who shared the intimate details of their internal operations so that others could learn how to serve customers better. Every one of you was responsive, caring, and a pleasure to interview. What you are helping us to bring to customer service will make a profound difference to businesses everywhere.

To our Mastermind group: Nancy Wellinger, Traci Armstrong, and Dawnaree Demrose. These colleagues and friends motivated, inspired, and supported us from the first time we said, "Let's write a book," through to the finish line.

To our friend and media expert Shawne Duperon, who believes that all things are possible, and our friend Martha Young from Clear Dialogue.

To Bob Nirkind, our gentle editor at AMACOM, who has guided us and offered great wisdom through the writing process, and John Willig of Literary Services, Inc., our agent, who saw the possibility of our vision and delighted us with his support.

To Maureen Monte of Empowered by Ethics, who generously read the very early chapters of the book and gave us valuable feedback.

Who's Your Gladys?

Introduction

When times are tough and customer dollars are scarce, it's the companies with exceptional customer service that weather the storm. If you want to keep customers coming back and happily recommending you to others, now is the time to ramp up your customer service to the highest possible level. Even when the economy gets back on track, those with extraordinary customer care enjoy the most profits.

Writing this book has been an adventure. We were a year into a recession, and the financial markets were melting down. Our hometown of Detroit saw two of its "Big Three" American automotive manufacturers ask the U.S. government for a bridge loan for billions of dollars. Companies all over the country were struggling to stay afloat. The timing for a book designed to help businesses retain their customers couldn't have been better.

We wrote *Who's Your Gladys? How to Turn Even Your Most Difficult Customer Into Your Biggest Fan* to uncover the vital secrets that thriving companies—small and large—know about customer service. Gladys is an actual customer (we've changed her name, of course) who appears in the first chapter of this book. As we heard more about her during our conversations with the managers of Professional Movers, one of the first companies that we interviewed, she became our poster child. Gladys represents that challenging client that all of us have encountered. Everyone in business has a Gladys or two—a customer or perhaps a coworker who requires a high level of skill to manage. Your Gladys may be a man, woman, or child. Your Gladys may be young or old. As you read our first chapter, we'd like to invite you to think of your Gladys as someone who can help you grow your business and your customer retention rate.

There's enough academic theory and "be nice" fluff out there; we wanted to give you substance—proven ways to keep your customers happy (so that they don't become Gladys) and turn even a hard-core Gladys into your biggest fan. We feature 10 companies, large and small, in a variety of industries. Every one of them has either experienced significant sales increases as a result of its customer care, won industry accolades for superior customer service, undergone a radical transformation that took its customer service to new levels, or taken an innovative approach that creates a bond of loyalty with its clients.

Here you'll find the stories of those companies, told to us by the fabulous, compassionate people who run them and by some of their empowered front-line employees. We gleaned a significant amount of immediately actionable information from these exceptional executives. They openly shared the inner workings of their organizations. They answered every question we asked. They told us about challenging situations, their unique customer service methods, and what they've learned from the mistakes they've made. We were amazed at their commitment to helping others by sharing their thoughts and recommendations so intimately.

While the companies that participated in this project come from different industries and have widely disparate methods, they have several core elements in common. Each of these organizations has an overall commitment to honoring its customers, its employees, and its vendors. All of them humanize the workplace and value customer relationships, focusing on providing a positive emotional experience. They value caring and kindness, rather than just getting the next dollar. (An abundance of wealth, higher rankings in your industry, and greater retention of high-quality staff are happy side effects of focusing on what really matters.)

These companies are dedicated to providing the best possible service to their customers, and they are steadfast in their efforts at continuous improvement. They do business with passion, with integrity, and in a way that generates goodwill. Their methods can be applied in any business, including yours. The best part? This book gives you concrete steps that you can take now to bring exceptional customer service to your company.

To help you benefit from what these extraordinary companies have told us, we've designed the chapters to tell their stories, pulling out crucial lessons and offering tools that you can use right now to transform both your personal approach and your company's customer satisfaction levels.

Every chapter gives you ways to make exceptional customer service a part of your company's unique personality. You'll find specific details that allow you to translate the information into immediate actions easily. For example, the Canfield Training Group shared how it manages workshops with hundreds of participants, some of whom make outrageous demands. It demonstrates how compassion solidifies client relationships, shows how tough love can be used to guide customer behavior, and offers an inspiring role model for emotion management skills in its director of training, Jesse Ianniello.

Another chapter focuses on Singapore Airlines, a global airline carrier that places a strong emphasis on delighting its customers by continually exceeding their expectations. Its employees are well trained and well managed. They love caring for their travelers in a way that makes even the longest transoceanic flight feel refreshing and worth an increased ticket price.

Whether you're starting at zero, halfway to fabulous, or going strong, you'll find practices that you can put into place immediately to take your customer service to the heights of exceptional. Continuous improvement is a hallmark of all exceptional companies. By applying the lessons you'll learn in this book, you'll join the ranks of those who are committed to growth and to higher levels of awareness and success.

And while you will learn many tactics for improving aspects of your business, there is also a vital personal growth aspect of customer service. Your efforts toward advancing your mood management and relationship skills will have a direct and significant impact on your professional growth. Throughout the book, you will find ways to grow your emotional competencies, gain new perspectives on the value of happiness, achieve life balance, and remain calm and compassionate during customers' tantrums and tirades. You'll see how you can translate mistakes into accelerated learning opportunities so that you actually improve the customer relationship as a result. What you don't know about emotion management and relationships, you can easily learn. (We've even put some personal growth resources at the end of the book so that you can keep learning after you've finished reading it.)

You'll be able to change both your mindset and your procedures by the time you've finished this book. And your Gladys will thank you for it.

Why Marilyn and Lori? Marilyn is the founder of Suttle Enterprises LLC and has taught thousands of people across the country how to have happier, more productive relationships with their customers, their colleagues, and even their children. Marilyn's parents were small business owners, as is her older brother. As a result, her appreciation for the customer connection was ingrained in her psyche at an early age. Her training business and speaking engagements allow her to live her dream of helping people to become more aware of their feelings so that they can generate life-balancing, success-inducing connections. She's created the

"Suttle Method" of communicating with compassion, teaching people how to use emotion management skills and inspiring audiences to savor their successes and connect in genuine, heartfelt ways.

Lori's background in sales and customer service management inspired her to teach others how to deliver compassionate service. As the manager of a successful teleproduction studio in metropolitan Detroit, her involvement in the day-to-day activities of a small business have allowed her to test the processes and recommendations you'll find in *Who's Your Gladys? How to Turn Even Your Most Difficult Customer Into Your Biggest Fan*. From the daily staff "morning huddle" meeting to the use of customer surveys and creative problem solving, she's using this information right now, growing the facility's revenue by 20 percent in 2008.

This book was born out of a desire to make a difference. Each of us had an interest in customer service, particularly the aspects of mood management and human compassion as well as the benefits of creating a personal connection with customers. More times than we could count, we would hear each other say, "I'd love to write a book to teach people the lessons I've learned." Then one day we looked at each other and said, "Let's do it!" We began meeting weekly, and the project took on a life of its own.

The people whose stories appear on these pages divinely showed up once we started looking for them. Some of the companies were on our radar from our day-to-day lives. After all, people talk about their horrible customer service experiences all the time. Wouldn't it be fun to tell the stories of fantastic experiences? We're both realistic optimists, so spreading great stories is one of our favorite pastimes. And if it can help someone else? That's even better!

Everyone that we approached to include in the book said yes to involvement in the project. They all gave us easy and quick access to their high-level executives and some of their front-line staff, who answered every question with a generous spirit and helpful information. While we had personally experienced how exceptional customer service requires compassion, a human connection, and strong relationships, it was inspiring to have that knowledge affirmed.

Researching and writing this book has been such a pleasure. As you read the pages ahead, please know how much we value you, our readers. We appreciate you for taking the time to meet Gladys and to explore our stories and lessons. We commend you for your desire to deliver exceptional customer service and grow your abilities. We wish you happy learning, stellar growth, and deep appreciation for your own customers.

CHAPTER 1

Professional Movers: Who's Your Gladys?

Professional Movers, a successful moving company in Walled Lake, Michigan, maintains a balanced approach to customer care by focusing on the details. We discovered several specific actions that are built into the company culture, an overall approach that has led to a dramatic 40 percent growth in sales in the last two years. What really stood out during our interviews with Director of Sales and Marketing Andrew Androff, one of the company's owners, was his genuine interest in the lives of his customers. He told us about Gladys, a difficult customer whose much-loved marble tabletop was broken by one of Andrew's movers. You'll discover the dramatic results that occurred because Andrew's sales rep Chris had paid attention to the details and taken the time to get to know his customer. Gladys is the embodiment of everyone's most challenging customer. She's the one who pushes your buttons and requires a higher degree of skill to manage. As you meet Gladys and the many other challenging customers throughout this book, we invite you to apply the lessons learned to your most difficult clients.

Eighty-seven-year-old Gladys has a reputation among her fellow retirement community members. She's known as a cranky complainer who is impossible to please. But to her surprise, when she called Andrew Androff's company, Professional Movers, to move her into her new apartment, she was treated with warmth and respect. When her sales rep, Chris, visited her home to quote the job, he noticed her prickly personality and made a conscious decision to focus on her spunk and tenacity. By the end of his visit, Gladys had bonded with Chris and booked the move.

On moving day, there was a mishap. One of the movers accidentally cracked Gladys's marble tabletop. Andrew knew that she would be furious. Determined to set things right, he prepared himself to let her vent before she could even think about possible solutions. As predicted, Gladys had steam shooting out her ears.

Andrew felt compassion for her while she vented and assured her that his company would have the table repaired, and that if she wasn't satisfied with the results, he would replace it. Although he continued to reassure her that things would be set right, she was still spitting mad. Gladys wanted to talk to Chris, who had sold her on the company in the first place, and Andrew promised to have Chris call her as soon as he came into the office.

Chris arrived dead tired after a long day filled with meetings with potential new customers. When Andrew told him about Gladys and asked if he'd be willing to call her, Chris responded, "No way. She's going to need more than a phone call. I'll stop by her house on my way home." Chris arrived at Gladys's house ready to comfort her through her anger and outrage. Then he assured her that he would personally oversee the repair of her table. This calmed her down, and she thanked him for coming over.

Unfortunately, the repair was less than perfect. Andrew knew that he had to set things right, even though doing so would be expensive. He called Gladys and promised that she could meet Chris at the marble store and personally pick out her new marble tabletop. Since Chris knew that Gladys didn't drive, he called and arranged to pick her up and take her to the store himself.

Gladys is now living at one of metropolitan Detroit's premier retirement communities with her new marble table. While it cost Andrew and his employee Chris extra time and extra money to make things right, the payoff was outstanding. Gladys tells everyone moving into or out of her assisted living complex that they have to hire Professional Movers if they want to work with the best movers in town. High and persistent praise from such a hard-to-please person attracts attention. As a result, Andrew's company is now the number one choice of movers for Gladys's retirement complex. By creating a culture that values compassionate connection with his customers, Andrew has built a referral base that has helped his sales grow by over 40 percent in two years.

This culture of connection has been particularly effective in building a strong business with senior citizens. Seniors often move from their homes to be nearer to their children or to retire to a senior community. Professional Movers has found this population to be a good fit for its particular style of customer service, so it put a great deal of effort into developing the market segment. Everyone at Professional Movers makes a practice of creating a human connection with her clients. The staff members show respect for their clients' wisdom, experience, and opinions. They also know how moving affects their clients, both physically and emotionally. It isn't easy leaving behind the security of their homes, their friendships with neighbors, and the familiarity of their routines. Andrew's employees are trained to be sensitive to the unique issues of downsizing. They are sensitive to the emotional connection to their precious family heirlooms that senior citizens feel as they leave behind the past. Professional Movers strives to give seniors the sort of service they would receive if their own family were doing the job.

"It's like we're their sons," Andrew said with a laugh. "We get very close with their families. We interview their caregivers and their social workers. It really helps us develop a customized process to address their concerns." This needs-based approach to both customer service and sales has helped the company become the top provider of moving services in metropolitan Detroit's retirement market.

HONORING YOUR CUSTOMERS' PREFERENCES PAYS OFF

Andrew gets to the heart of customized customer service for all his market segments. Another fast-growing category for Professional Movers is Japanese nationals. Andrew's business is located in an area that has seen an evolving community of Japanese automotive executives over the last decade. As he began working with them, he saw that many of the Japanese automotive engineers were being bombarded with new customs and sometimes overwhelmed as they adapted to the American way of life. While connecting with this market, he and his employees researched Japanese traditions and spoke to their Japanese prospects about their unique cultural perspective. Now, every staffer who enters a Japanese family's home will take his shoes off and put on clean footies. The employees also move the furniture the way it is traditionally done in Japan, using different packing methods from those used in the United States. Even though it takes a bit longer, it makes the client feel better, happier, and more relaxed to see things measured and boxed the way it's done in their home country. As a result, Professional Movers is also the top referral company for executives moving into the area from Japan.

PAYING CLOSE ATTENTION TO CUSTOMERS' NEEDS MAKES A DIFFERENCE

Here's one more example of how Professional Movers recognizes and honors a growing population of customers with special needs. Andrew went out to quote a move for an elderly man with Parkinson's disease. He felt an instant connection with this customer. As they walked through the house, the man shared that his wife had been bedridden for years and asked Andrew to go in and meet her. She was a frail waif of a woman, barely 80 pounds. When Andrew introduced himself, the tiny woman pointed at him and said, "Do a good job or I'll kick your ass!" Fending off laughter, Andrew assured her that he would put his best men on the job.

As Andrew completed his initial walk through the home, he noticed a massive armoire in the bedroom. He knew that it was too big for two workers to move by themselves. He also knew that adding a third man just to help the crew with one large chest would increase the cost of the move, which would be a further burden on a couple who had more than their share of financial concerns. "Don't worry," he promised his customer. "On my way to the office, I'll stop here and help the guys put your armoire onto the truck. They can handle the rest of the job by themselves, and I'll only have to charge you for two movers."

On the day of the move, Andrew showed up early. He greeted his client and helped to move the armoire. As he was about to leave, he noticed that the man seemed concerned. That's when Andrew said, "I'm leaving you with two of our best and most intelligent movers." The man's face brightened, as did the faces of his movers. Andrew said that it's rare that a moving professional is called intelligent, although in reality it takes both knowledge and experience to maneuver expensive furniture quickly and efficiently. It also takes customer service savvy to keep the customers coming back and referring their friends and family members.

"Our employees follow rigorous guidelines for getting detailed information and then addressing the needs they uncover," Andrew explained. "They are thoroughly trained on both moving skills and customer service skills. They know it's their job to make the customers' lives easier. We learn about our clients. What are they doing? What do they need to think about? Are they downsizing? Is there urgency to the move? We need to learn as much as possible about their situation before we show up to do the job. And in the end, the time spent up front pays off in a big way in how happy our clients are with us and how comfortable they are referring their friends and relatives."

Everyone who hires a moving company has his own specific needs. One customer may have a cherished heirloom, and needs reassurance that it will be handled by experts and arrive at the next location intact. Another customer may be downsizing after having lived in her home for 30 years. She needs emotional support and help in disposing of her excess belongings. Still other customers may have cultural customs that they wish to have honored in a company's dealings with them, or have special needs and require reassurance that the job will be handled with care. By tuning in to each customer's unique needs, Andrew creates a connection that keeps his clients coming back for more, recommending him to others, and raising his company's level of success.

*   *   *

Now that you've read the case study for Professional Movers, how will you take what Andrew has done and apply it to your company? Read through the Practical Points, Progress Checklist, and Lessons Learned sections that follow and notice which ideas you are already putting to use in your own business and which ones you can adopt. Then set a goal for paying attention to the details of your customers' needs.

PRACTICAL POINTS

Point 1: Customer service is about seeing the positive qualities in a client with negative behavior.

Gladys could easily be described as a chronic complainer or a demanding old woman. Instead, Chris saw her as spunky and tenacious. When you look for the positive qualities of your challenging customer, you increase your ability to connect with that customer and enjoy your time together. Here's a list that can help you translate negative behavioral traits into positive qualities. How you think about your customers influences how you respond to them. When you begin noticing the positive qualities, your clients will start responding to you differently, because how you act is determined by how you think.

Pushy or demanding	Knows what he wants
Argumentative	Eager to debate possibilities
Complaining	Sharing what she doesn't want
Rude	Willing to say what's on his mind
Slow	Deliberate
Cold	Private person who takes time to establish trust
Obnoxious	Intelligent person who feels underappreciated
Cranky	Tenacious
Loud	Bold
Intimidating	Wants more respect and authority
Cheap	Fearful of being separated from her money

Point 2: Customer service is about feeling compassion while your customers vent their emotions.

When customers yell, they aren't yelling at you. They are yelling at the company. It isn't personal, but it sure feels like it is. Is it possible to feel good or calm or compassionate instead? Yes, because the truth is that your customers' complaints need to be heard before they can focus on positive solutions.

Psychologists tell us that good feelings cannot be restored until bad feelings are released. It's like turning on a hot water faucet. The water from the faucet doesn't begin to feel warm until the water that has been sitting in the pipes has flowed out. Andrew knew that getting angry with Gladys would prevent her from releasing her anger and moving forward. Even though his offer to repair the table, and even to replace it if she wasn't satisfied, was above and beyond what other companies might do, he didn't expect her to be happy right away. He honored her process of coping with her loss. He understood that he might feel the same way if he were in her shoes.

Your customers may have had life experiences that taught them to have a hostile reaction to bad news. By focusing on giving clients what they need—someone to listen to them—you move them toward resolution, and it gives you a role to hang on to during the storm.

Point 3: Customer service is about getting to know and love your customers.

How did Chris know that Gladys doesn't drive? He treated her like a person instead of a transaction. He talked with her, not at her. He asked questions and began building a relationship with her right from the start. People are interesting. Develop a curiosity about them, and you will enrich not only their lives, but yours as well. Instead of asking yourself, "What don't I like about this client?" ask yourself, "What do I know, admire, and respect about this client?"

Point 4: Customer service is about giving your customers what they need.

Although Chris is a young man who probably doesn't have a lot in common with an 87-year-old woman, he was able to ask himself, "What does my customer need?" Because he took the time to get to know Gladys, it was easier for him to meet her needs. Driving the extra miles to Gladys's house may seem excessive, but he knew that she would calm down more quickly with in-person reassurances from someone she trusted.

As much as Chris gives his customers what they need, he also gets what he needs from Andrew, one of the owners of Professional Movers. Andrew's appreciation goes a long way, letting Chris know that his actions are having a positive effect on the company.

Point 5: Customer service is about taking care in the details of your everyday actions.

The 40 percent growth in Professional Movers's sales came from all the care that Andrew and his staff put into the details of their business day. They don't just meet new clients; they get to know new people. They don't just work a new market segment; they work on understanding the needs of that segment. They don't just move furniture; they help people feel comfortable before, during, and after they move into their new home.

Point 6: Customer service is about seeing challenging situations as opportunities to strengthen the customer relationship.

No company is perfect. Mistakes will happen. How your customers feel about your company after a mistake depends on how you handle it. If everything had gone right, Gladys would have been satisfied and might not have had a lot to say. When the mistake was handled with tender, loving care, Gladys had nothing but good things to say, and she said them to everyone.

Referral business brings success. When your efforts are the cause of referral business, you know you have developed skills that will increase your revenue. Increase your business abilities—and your customer service skills—by seeing every difficult situation as an opportunity to strengthen your relationship with your customer.

Point 7: Customer service is about honoring the customs of your customers.

Take the time to learn about and respond to the customs of your customers. This can be as easy as asking a few questions, doing an Internet search, or bringing up the topic at a staff meeting. The more respect you show for people's differences, the more your business and your skills will grow.

PROGRESS CHECKLIST

As you read the following checklist, rate yourself on a scale from one to ten. Are you applying the lessons you learned from Professional Movers? What can you do today to bring your customer service up a notch in each category?

> 1–2–3–4–5–6–7–8–9–10
> _____ See the positive quality of a client's negative behavior.
> _____ Feel compassion while your customers vent their emotions.
> _____ Get to know and care about your customers.
> _____ Give your customers what they need.
> _____ Put care into the details of your everyday actions.
> _____ View challenging situations as opportunities to make the client relationship even stronger.
> _____ Honor the customs of your customers.

LESSONS LEARNED

The story of Professional Movers presents plenty of examples of how paying attention to the details allows you to provide the absolute best customer service. To help you identify and develop concrete skills based on this case study, read through the following questions. Answer each one for yourself before reading our responses to see how much understanding you've already gained.

1. How do you handle an abrasive customer who is pushing all your buttons?

   _____

   _____

   _____

   _____

   _____

2. What helps stressed-out customers relax and develop trust in your company?

   _____

   _____

   _____

   _____

   _____

3. What is the most direct way to find out how to make your customers' lives easier?

   _____

   _____

   _____

   _____

   _____

4. What is one thing that you can be sure is the same about all customers?

   _____

   _____

   _____

   _____

   _____

5. How do you address your customers' emotional concerns?

_____

_____

_____

_____

_____

6. How can your company become a customer favorite?

_____

_____

_____

_____

_____

7. How do you show that you care for your internal customers?

_____

_____

_____

_____

_____

ANSWERS

1. **How do you handle an abrasive customer who is pushing all your buttons?**

   Show her even more care. Sometimes the more challenging customers can turn out to be your biggest, most vocal supporters. It's common knowledge that when children act their worst, that's when they need their parents' love the most. Customers who are acting their worst may have a lot of fear or distrust that has nothing to do with you and everything to do with their life experiences. When you depersonalize abrasive behavior and see it as a call for help, you become a catalyst for the best kind of change. Look for the positive qualities in your clients' negative behavior.

2. **What helps stressed-out customers relax and develop trust in your company?**

   Customers want to know that their needs will be met. Become aware of your customers' expectations and concerns, and let them know what you will do. Reassure them and take action. Putting your customers' fears to rest helps them relax and work with you, instead of against you.

3. **What is the most direct way to find out how to make your customers' lives easier?**

   Ask questions. Not sure what questions to ask? Tap into your curiosity. Start by asking yourself, "What information would allow me to be more helpful to this person?" Look back at Andrew's story. What questions do you suppose the people at Professional Movers ask to help them to better understand the special needs of their customers?

4. **What is one thing that you can be sure is the same about all customers?**

   What all customers have in common is that each one is unique. Customers have different needs. They each have different concerns, desires, and personal histories that affect the way they act and what they want from you. When you listen for and seek out the specific needs, concerns, and feelings of each customer, you create a connection that brings about the best possible results.

5. **How do you address your customers' emotional concerns?**

   Notice what your customers' stress points are, and let them know what you will do about them. Andrew did this when he said, "I'm leaving you with two of our best and most intelligent movers." Chris did this when he personally drove to the customer's house to offer reassurance.

6. **How can your company become a customer favorite?**

   Authentic interest in your customers creates uncommon success. When you know what customers need and you respond accordingly, you create a connection that keeps you in their minds and contact lists for years.

7. **How do you show that you care for your internal customers?**

   Andrew's employees are the company's internal customers, and he treats them with the same warmth and appreciation that he gives to his external customers. To create a sense of fun and enjoyment in their work, Andrew even bought company T-shirts that say, "Relax, I'm a Professional" and "We promise fast service, no matter how long it takes," along with other fun sayings, with the company name on the back. The "I'm a Professional" shirts are by far the most popular. When employees wear them, they *feel* and *act* like professionals.

WHO'S YOUR GLADYS?

The odds are good that at some time or another, you've had a customer like Gladys. You may even have one on your current client roster. Can you find something about her or him to appreciate? How are you going to respond to your Gladys so that she can become your most vocal ambassador?

CHAPTER 2

The Canfield Companies: Where's My Refrigerator?

The Canfield Training Group is a highly profitable company in the self-help field, teaching entrepreneurs, educators, corporate leaders, and employees to achieve their personal and professional goals. The company's CEO, Jack Canfield, was one of the original founders of Chicken Soup for the Soul Enterprises. Among his many amazing accomplishments, he holds the Guinness world record as the author of seven books that appeared on the New York Times best-seller list simultaneously. We discovered that the employees of the Canfield Training Group "walk the talk," doing what it takes to manage their emotions no matter how challenging things get. They take optimal care of their customers, consistently offering compassion to even the most difficult ones. We were particularly impressed by Jesse Ianniello, the company's director of training. She uses her well-honed customer service skills to respond to the crazy schedules and demanding requests of the company's inquisitive customers. She knows how to keep her cool, even when one seminar participant made an unlikely request involving a mini refrigerator.

Imagine this. You work for Jack Canfield, the world-famous expert in the personal growth field, known as America's Number One Success Coach. He was the founder of Chicken Soup for the Soul Enterprises, a billion-dollar empire, and more recently was the author of the inspirational best seller *The Success Principles*. He was also featured on the best-selling DVD *The Secret*. You are his director of training, responsible for registering hundreds of people each year for programs that cost thousands of dollars. Your e-mail inbox is full, and your phone never stops ringing. People want to take the training, but they have tons of questions that need to be answered before they register. You are the person responsible for answering all those questions.

After they register for the training, your customers have even more questions—about the hotel, the food, the agenda, and how to dress. The list goes on and on. It's not unusual for you to receive up to 50 e-mails from a single individual over the six months leading up to a workshop. Multiply that by the hundreds who register and you have one busy schedule. And that's only one part of your job description.

You also secure the hotel accommodations for the Canfield staff, arrange special hotel rates for the attendees, prepare and ship the books and materials for the courses, coordinate everyone's schedules, and scope out venues for future training courses. Once you arrive at the workshop location, you wear many hats. You are the go-to person for the hotel staff. You head up the back-of-the-room book sales. You track the payment and registration of hundreds of participants. In addition to several other pressing tasks, you have a line of participants at every break waiting to ask you questions, and all the while the hotel staff is pulling on your arm to confirm meal arrangements. In spite of this crazy schedule, though, the most remarkable thing about your work is the incredibly positive reaction that customers have toward you. As they arrive at the hotel, participants seek you out to personally thank you for all the help you've given them. They treat you like a superstar. When you are introduced on the first day of the training, you receive a standing ovation. How would it feel to receive that kind of response from your customers?

Just ask Jesse Ianniello. She is the director of training for Jack Canfield's companies, which include the Canfield Training Group and Self-Esteem Seminars, Inc. A 27-year-old dynamo, Jesse is a master of positive customer interactions, taking the time to answer customer questions thoroughly, no matter how busy she is at the time. It's an approach that pays off, as it did on the last day of a weeklong training program. One participant took Jesse aside and said, "If you hadn't explained this training the way you did, I wouldn't have come. I don't know how to thank you. I have three homes in Mexico, and any time you want, you can bring your friends or family and stay there. Just tell me when you're coming."

Jesse had developed a six-month relationship with this participant before the training program. She patiently answered all his questions and addressed all his concerns so that he could see for himself that the program would meet his needs.

CUSTOMERS RESPOND TO COMPASSION AND CALM

When asked about the Canfield Training Group's view of its customers, the company president, Patty Aubery, said, "They always come first. Our mission statement is to help people grow to live their highest vision in the context of love and joy. And our commitment to them is to deliver only the best products, training, and content available. I like to think that we overdeliver each time we interact with our students, clients, and vendors, for that matter." "Service means just that," Jack Canfield added. "We're in business to serve people, not ourselves."

One of the keys to Jesse's success with customers is her compassion. It's part of the company culture. When asked how he would sum up his approach to customer service, Jack replied, "Treat people with love. Put yourself in the customer's shoes. Treat people the way you want to be treated." And that's exactly what Jesse does in every interaction she has with any of her clients.

During a typical break in a seminar, she has five or six people waiting to ask her questions about anything from signing up for future training to receiving alternative vegetarian lunch options. At the same time, she has hotel staff members asking her to help coordinate services, while other staff members break in to ask, "Where are the coaching sign-up forms?" It's enough to stress out even the calmest human being, but not Jesse. She talks with each individual as if he were the only person in the room. She doesn't rush anyone. She doesn't even look shocked when a participant makes an unexpected request, like the time a man asked for a mini refrigerator so that he could eat cold snacks throughout the session. Instead, Jesse calmly answers people's questions, provides reassurance, and gives them whatever guidance they need, one at a time, until she reaches the end of the line. And what about the refrigerator? Jesse found out that the hotel would supply one without charge, so she honored the man's request.

"Unless something is urgent, like the kitchen is on fire, it's easier to handle what comes up right at that time," she explained. "I don't like to make a long to-do list. If something can be easily answered, I handle it right then. It's the quickest way to move through things."

Jesse joined Canfield's organization as an intern midway through her senior year of college. Upon graduation, she was hired full-time as a receptionist. "I learned the most about the company as the receptionist. Answering phones and opening mail gave me a chance to learn who everyone was and how things worked," she said.

When hiring new employees, the leaders of the Canfield Training Group teach them exactly what is expected. "At our company, we want everyone—both employees and customers—to be treated well. We want to be the Nordstrom[1] of personal development," Patty explained.

Jesse came into the Canfield organization with no previous customer service training, although she credits her parents with teaching her basics that apply to her current position. "They taught me that everyone's different. Everyone comes from a different background, and that doesn't make anyone better than someone else. They also taught me to treat everyone with kindness."

Her parents' influence helped her fit into the personal development and customer service culture that serves as the foundation of all of Jack Canfield's companies. In fact, Robert Spector, author of the acclaimed business book *Lessons from the Nordstrom Way: How Companies Are Emulating the #1 Customer Service Company*,[2] interviewed Bruce Nordstrom, a man known to hire for attitude instead of sales skills. When asked, "Who really trains the salespeople?" Nordstrom answered, "Their parents." When it comes to hiring, the Canfield Training Group places a high priority on the proper attitude.

"I love to start with young people who have a positive attitude and the self-esteem required to believe that anything is possible," Patty shared. "I look for bright young talent that is energetic and positive. I feel that if they have the 'whatever it takes' attitude, they can learn the skills, and with good leadership, they will gain the experience." The Canfield Training Group is a small company, so Aubery has the opportunity to rotate staffers through different departments to see what will fit them best.

"Many people go through life settling for just a 'job.' Our environment allows them to discover their talents. From there, I like to help them build on those talents and take them to the highest level."

Jesse may have learned how to be kind and attentive from her parents, but she learned how to be calm in the storm from a coworker, Veronica

Romero. Veronica's been with the company for more than 12 years and moved through several positions before landing her spot as Jack's executive assistant. She became a role model to Jesse because of the exceptional way she manages her emotions under pressure. "I learned a lot about how to stay calm in the storm from her," explained Jesse. "It can be crazy here, but she's never freaked out. She is calm in everything she does. She leads by example and gets the job done, even when it's hectic. She really follows Jack's teaching that getting worked up isn't going to add to the goal of getting things done; it just makes things worse."

"I think the most important thing you can do as an employer is to be available to guide employees through stressful, busy, and sometimes trying times," Patty added. "This is where they get to see that persistence is key and that if they stick with it and keep on keeping on, they can achieve their goals."

Patty Aubery likes to give her employees continuous feedback, both positive and negative, and acknowledge success frequently. "I think that—more than anything—people want to know that their work and their loyalty are appreciated and noticed. Most of our employees stay on for a very long time due to the environment that we help create *with* them. They are also compensated well and are given bonuses at the end of the year based on the profits of the company. It creates a great sense of team, knowing that if they work together, they share in the profits."

The transformational nature of Canfield's training shows up in the way his company is run. Even though employees have official titles, no one is pigeonholed in a particular role. Employees are encouraged to do what they are capable of, and interested in, doing. Jesse had always shown interest in and aptitude for the training area of the company, so when an opening became available, she was put in charge. "I'm lucky," she said. "Jack says to find what you like to do and what you're good at, then everything will make sense and opportunities will show up. That's what's happened for me."

EMPATHY CALMS A CONCERNED CUSTOMER

A few years ago, a registered seminar participant called Jesse a couple of weeks before the training program to cancel. She was a stay-at-home mother, and she had listened to one of the training preview calls, which are advance teleconferences that describe the benefits of the upcoming Canfield training. She felt that her focus on her family meant that she wouldn't be a worthy participant in the training. It was Jesse's job to help the woman get her needs met, and she knew just what to do. Using a technique that she finds continually helpful, she mentally put herself in the woman's place. "If it were me on the phone, I'd want someone to talk to me honestly and take time with me," she explained. "These people are spending a lot of time and energy and money to be here. If it were me, that's how I would want to be treated."

While most people are excited after the preview call, this woman said, "I do not belong at this training. There are going to be a lot of businesspeople there, and I'm just a housewife. I don't have anything to offer everyone."

"Of course you have something to offer," Jesse responded. "There are going to be other people just like you at the training. You'll have things to offer to people who don't know what it's like to stay at home and take care of a family."

Jesse helped the woman see her value, and she chose to attend the training. That reluctant housewife sought Jesse out at the workshop to give her a big hug and thank her. "I wouldn't have come if it hadn't been for you," she said. Her husband agreed. "I'm so happy you talked to her," he said. "It's really good that she's here."

Jesse's empathy for customers helps to explain why the number one question the staff hears during workshop registration is, "Where is Jesse?" People can't wait to introduce themselves to the woman who gave them such great attention as they went through their decision-making process.

If it seems as if Jesse is practically perfect in every way, she's the first one to tell you it isn't so. "I make mistakes," she laughed. When she started with the company, she fumbled a bit while learning the system, running credit cards when she shouldn't have or patching people directly through to Jack without following the system. "Here no one beats you up when you make a mistake. It's a learning experience; they tell you how to do it right, then you do it right," she added. She sees mistakes as a form of accelerated learning.

"Knowing that I don't know everything and being okay with that is what's gotten me where I am. I didn't come in knowing everything. I think that's why I'm able to learn, because I know I don't know every-thing. So, I'm really willing to learn how to do it and improve what I'm doing. I want to learn skills about business and companies. I really like to learn; it excites me. I love to do new things."

A SPOONFUL OF KINDNESS HELPS WHEN GIVING TOUGH LOVE

Sometimes customers need tough love. For Jack Canfield, and anyone else who presents programs to customers, the needs of the group sometimes outweigh the needs of an individual.

Have you ever been to a meeting and noticed a spike of hostility in the room when someone's cell phone went off? The trainer loses her point, the audience loses its concentration, and if the person answers it and begins talking, those who are close by can't hear what's happening in the front of the room. Some trainers go out of their way to punish a person whose cell phone goes off to make an example of him. That only creates anxiety and discomfort in the room.

Jack's approach eliminates hostility and transforms the way people react to the occasional cell phone interruption. At the beginning of his weeklong training, he tells everyone to silence his cell phone. But he doesn't stop there. Knowing that there will always be someone who needs to be in contact with work or home, he gives out the phone number of one of his assistants to be used as an emergency number.

He then says, "If your cell phone goes off during the training, I will expect you to hand over 20 dollars." There's always a moment of shocked silence, then he tells people that the money will be donated to a charity. One time, it went toward building an orphanage in Bali. Another time, money was collected to help dig wells in an African village.

When the inevitable happens and someone's cell phone rings, the designated collector of the donations comes running to collect the money. Instead of hostility, everyone feels happy, knowing that good is being done. At the same time, the number of cell phones going off during the week decreases dramatically.

Jack's creative approach to healthy boundaries pays off in many ways. On the last day of the training, there always seems to be a group of participants who arrange a burst of cell phone rings to collect more donation money. One year, $16,000 was raised for a charitable cause in a matter of 15 minutes, as participants rallied together to boost the amount collected from ringing cell phones. This form of creative problem solving creates a positive experience for everyone, while efficiently managing a persistent customer issue.

* * *

Now that you've read the case study for the Canfield Training Group, see if you can apply what the people who work there do at your company. Read through the Practical Points, Progress Checklist, and Lessons Learned sections that follow and notice which ideas you are already putting to use in your own business and which ones you can adopt. Then set a goal for giving your customers more compassion and kindness in the days ahead.

PRACTICAL POINTS

Point 1: Customer service is about being fully present.

No matter what background, financial status, or title your customers have, they are, at the most basic level, human beings. When you take the time to give them your undivided attention, they feel validated. If you're feeling stressed, take care of yourself and you will be better able to care for your customers. (Don't forget, it's not the customer's job to take care of your needs, it's yours!) Take a walk to clear your head. Take a few deep breaths and calm yourself before responding so that you can give your full attention to your customers when they need you.

Point 2: Customer service is about finding value in the lessons learned from mistakes.

Some people feel uncomfortable when they know that they don't know something. That discomfort comes from a fear of looking bad or getting into trouble. What would it be like to be comfortable with knowing that you don't know? That's the first step toward learning something new. When there's something new to learn, get excited about it. Love to learn and you'll love the results you get on the job. View mistakes the way Jesse does, as a form of accelerated learning.

Point 3: Customer service is about empathizing with your customers.

Empathy goes further than just being nice. It requires you to disengage from your own opinions and points of view long enough to imagine what the customer is experiencing. That allows you to respond with compassion, whether or not you agree with the customer. Getting in touch with what the customer feels, needs, or wishes will go a long way toward creating the kind of connection that strengthens relationships and produces lifelong customers.

Point 4: Customer service is about picking a role model who has the qualities you want to develop.

Do you know someone who stays calm during hectic times? Whether it's someone you work with, know of, or read about, having a role model will help to reinforce the behaviors you wish to adopt. Imagine what kind of results you would get if you were to give 5 percent more attention to remaining calm during hectic times. It's helpful to ask yourself, "How would my role model handle this?" or, better yet, look to your future self and ask: "How would the customer service provider I know I can be handle the situation I'm about to handle?"

Point 5: Customer service is about meeting unique needs.

It is easy to get flustered and dismiss requests that seem bizarre or unusual. It may even be tempting to roll your eyes at the more zany requests. However, before you decline or dismiss a request, give yourself a moment to consider what it would take to grant it. Would it be possible, given your time and resources? What might it mean to your customer? With compassion, you become more resourceful.

Marilyn volunteered to sit behind a registration desk at one of Jack Canfield's trainings. A participant asked if it would be possible to locate the digital picture that was taken of her for the class directory and e-mail it to her. It seemed like a strange request, and Marilyn had a list of other things to do. Marilyn put her off by taking her name and leaving a note for Robert, the team captain, just in case he had extra time later in the day. Instead, Robert asked Marilyn if she would take care of it. It took her all of two minutes to get online, upload the picture, and fill in the e-mail address.

Later that day, the woman who made the request gave Marilyn a hug, saying, "That's the best picture that's ever been taken of me. Thank you so much." Marilyn was relieved that she hadn't dismissed the woman, and she realized that she could have both saved time and made the customer happy sooner if she had taken the request more seriously up front.

Point 6: Customer service is about establishing trust.

Your integrity is crucial in helping customers determine whether your company's products and services will meet their needs. When customers trust that you have their best interests at heart, they fall in love with your company. Take the time to explore the needs of your customers and give them honest answers to their questions to establish trust. Even when you can't do exactly what they want, being straightforward about what you can do and working to come up with the right solution for them will pay off.

Point 7: Customer service is about answering repetitive questions graciously.

Customers don't know that others have asked you the exact same question hundreds of times before. And, of course, there will be times when one customer will ask the same question repeatedly. His intention is not to irritate you, but to comfort himself. Customers sometimes need reassurance and confirmation before they feel comfortable doing business with your company. Challenge yourself to answer each question as if it were the first time you've heard it. If you're corresponding by e-mail, make copies of your answers to frequently asked questions to reduce the effort it takes to respond and speed up your reply.

PROGRESS CHECKLIST

As you read the following checklist, rate yourself on a scale from one to ten. Are you applying the lessons learned from Jesse and the Canfield Training Group? What can you do today to bring your compassion up a notch in each category?

1–2–3–4–5–6–7–8–9–10
_____ Be fully present.
_____ Value and learn from your mistakes.
_____ Empathize with your customers.
_____ Pick a role model with the qualities you want to develop.
_____ Meet unique customer needs.
_____ Establish trust.
_____ Answer repetitive questions graciously.

LESSONS LEARNED

The story of Jesse Ianniello and the Canfield organization presents many ways to take a compassionate approach to attract and retain customers, especially during trying times. To help you pinpoint these empathetic skills and make them a part of your everyday practice, read through the following questions. Answer each one for yourself before reading our responses to see how much understanding you've already gained.

1. What does paying attention have to do with compassionate customer service?

    _____

    _____

    _____

    _____

    _____

2. What do I do if I don't know how to solve a customer service issue?

    _____

    _____

    _____

    _____

3. How can I be more empathetic to my customers?

    _____

    _____

    _____

    _____

4. What is the best approach to dealing with unusual customer requests?

    _____

    _____

    _____

    _____

5. When hiring customer service staff, should I hire for attitude over aptitude?

    _____

    _____

    _____

    _____

6. Where does customer service start?

    _____

    _____

    _____

    _____

    _____

7. How do I provide "calm in the storm" for my customers?

    _____

    _____

    _____

    _____

    _____

ANSWERS

1. **What does paying attention have to do with compassionate customer service?**

    Jesse represents the Canfield organization to customers, and when she treats people with care and genuine interest, they fall in love with both her and the company. Treating people with respect, kindness, and attention isn't hard, but it takes focus. Jesse focuses on each and every customer as a unique individual. The focus you put on your customers will pay off in loyalty and repeat business.

2. **What do I do if I don't know how to solve a customer service issue?**

    Acknowledge that you don't know how to solve it, then work quickly to find the answer. Most clients don't mind hearing "I'll have to check with my boss" as long as they know you're truly trying to help them. Having the right customer service attitude is the most important step toward success. Learning how to put solid customer service techniques into action is next. Always be open to learning new things about your business and about customer service. No one knows everything, and continual learning—asking questions, reading books, attending seminars, doing role-playing exercises with your team—will lead to inevitable success.

3. **How can I be more empathetic to my customers?**

    Imagining yourself in your customer's shoes is one of the best ways to figure out how to give her what she needs. If you received an invoice that wasn't what you expected it to be, would you be a bit angry? If so, then you can understand the anger in your client's voice when he calls to tell you that his billing didn't match his expectations. Would you get stressed out if your boss was demanding that you meet an impossible deadline? Then you can imagine how a customer feels when she has to ask you to rush a project through for her. Jesse's empathy with the customer who felt inadequate because she was "only a housewife" allowed her to meet the woman's need for a boost of self-esteem. And it made all the difference for the customer and for her husband.

4.   **What is the best approach to dealing with unusual customer requests?**

The key is to remain calm and attentive. Jesse takes time to hone in on every customer and his unique needs. She focuses her attention on each individual, responding to his questions as if he were the only person in the room, then making sure that his needs are met. Paying strict attention to her customers shows them that they're important and that she cares about their unique requests, no matter how unusual they might be. If a customer calls you with an odd request, stand back and think before you say no. Perhaps meeting that request might be possible with minimal extra effort—effort that could pay off in a stronger client relationship.

5.   **When hiring customer service staff, should I hire for attitude over aptitude?**

Yes! Jesse came to the Canfield organization with a great attitude, which made it easier for her to learn the compassionate approach that's an integral part of the company's makeup. Customer service stars know that hiring for attitude is an important part of creating a customer-friendly culture. Hiring people who have a positive outlook on life can be challenging, although there are interview questions and interview testing tools that can help you determine if your potential new hire sees the glass as "half full" or "half empty."

6.   **Where does customer service start?**

Customer service starts from the inside out. What's happening on the inside eventually shows up on the outside. Give your internal customers (everyone who benefits from the work you do *inside* the company) the instructions and resources they need in order to succeed. Treat them with the same respect and good treatment that you give your external customers. When employees feel appreciated and capable, they will naturally respond to your customers in a more positive way.

7.   **How do I provide "calm in the storm" for my customers?**

Have you ever gone into a busy store and felt like the cashier was rushing you through the checkout lane, forgetting to say "please" and "thank you"? How did it make you feel? Most customers want to feel important, and being rushed conveys several things—including disorganization, lax service, and, most of all, stress. By calmly walking through their to-do list, Veronica and Jesse convey mastery to their customers. No worries here; these women aren't stressed out at all, so they must have it all under control. The calm you feel gives your customers permission to relax and trust you.

WHO'S YOUR GLADYS?

The next time one of your customers asks for her version of a mini refrigerator, how could you respond with compassion? Imagine how happy she would be if you honored her request.

NOTES

1. Patty is referring to Nordstrom, the specialty store offering apparel and accessories for men, women, and children that is lauded for its excellent customer service.

2. *"Lessons from the Nordstrom Way: How Companies Are Emulating the #1 Customer Service Company" by Robert Spector, New York: John Wiley & Sons, Inc.*

CHAPTER 3

Paul Reed Smith Guitars: Starting from Scratch

Paul Reed Smith Guitars (PRS) manufactures high-end instruments that are played by rock stars, coveted by collectors, and enjoyed by enthusiasts around the world. In an industry where competing brands have been in existence for centuries, this relatively new kid on the block, founded in 1985, has earned its place in guitar-making history with a gold standard for quality. Its success is due to the spectacular beauty and sound of its guitars and the passion that PRS people put into their work. Throughout the company, we found a commitment to service that is so enthusiastic that customers have created fan club forums on the Internet to rave about both the products and the people there who take care of their needs. When we spoke to guitar-building icon Paul Reed Smith and his senior-level managers, we discovered highly passionate professionals with a heartfelt desire to bring the best possible instruments to life for their customers. That passion translates into happy customers who love both the guitars and the company itself. In this chapter, you'll discover how a scratched guitar case set off a chain of events that startled and pleased an irate customer.

When his customers complain, Shawn Nuthall, manager of customer service at Paul Reed Smith Guitars, feels their pain. How he responds to that pain has created extreme customer loyalty and caused guitarists to sing his praises through online guitar forums all over the Internet. Shawn simply cannot tolerate having customers jump through hoops to get their issues resolved. He is passionate about getting problems handled in the most painless way possible, so he manages the issues himself.

In one instance, an irate customer called Shawn, fuming with frustration. He had purchased a PRS guitar from an online dealer, and when he pulled it out of the shipping box, he had discovered a six-inch scratch on the case. The angry customer was sure that the scratch was caused by the long staples that were used to seal the packaging. The dealer would not take responsibility for the damage, insisting that the case was in perfect condition when it was shipped out. Without a moment's hesitation, Shawn took the most immediate approach to resolving his customer's issue. He said, "What's your address? I'll send you out a new case." Relieved, the customer asked, "What do you want me to do with the damaged case?" Shawn replied, "Maybe you can pay it forward and help out a kid who needs a case. If not, consider it a backup, and when you go to your next gig, take the beat-up case."

The customer was shocked, "That's it? You're just going to send me a case?" Shawn didn't see a reason to put his customer to any further trouble. "He had a problem, and I took care of it. If I have a problem with a product, I want to call the company and have it handled quickly. It doesn't serve me to give people the runaround. If someone calls with a problem and I can make that problem go away painlessly, why wouldn't I? I don't understand the philosophy of companies that expect you to make 10 different phone calls and talk to 20 different people." Shawn's approach turned his angry customer into a fan, and soon afterward, Paul Reed Smith himself received a glowing letter about this guitarist's extreme satisfaction with Shawn and with PRS.

CUSTOMERS AREN'T PROBLEMS, THEY'RE PEOPLE

Employees in all positions within PRS are allowed significant latitude in straightening out their customers' issues. "I have a lot of flexibility to solve problems, so I try to figure out what's motivating the customer and what is behind her anger," said Shawn. "Some people just want to be recognized or made to feel special. Basically, it is a negotiation. We have some rules and guidelines we like to follow as far as what is covered under warranty, but I want to figure out what it is they want to accomplish." The company founder, Paul Reed Smith, has been a role model for Shawn. "We treat people the way we want to be treated," Paul explained. "That's all there is to it."

Shawn is quick to say, "I don't have any enlightened answer. I put myself in their position. When I hear, 'Look, I just spent three thousand dollars on a guitar and this doesn't work or that doesn't work,' I ask myself, how would I feel if it were me? I would ask, 'Hey, will you make this problem go away?'" Shawn's words probably won't make it on a motivational calendar, but they pretty much say it all: "A customer is not a problem on the phone, he's a person."

Shawn answers up to 500 e-mails a week as well as numerous phone calls with requests like, "I'm interested in your guitars. Can you tell me more about them?" or "I bought a used guitar and want to confirm the serial number for it," or "I love the guitar, but I'd like to get some pickups that make it sound more vintage." He also gets calls from customers with warranty issues.

"I encourage Shawn to tell me when he can't do it alone so I can add another person," said his team leader, the director of marketing at PRS, Peter Wolf. "Adding another person isn't necessarily something that a CFO would want to do because it costs money, but at the end of the day, if you have 500 people out there who are happy, you need only one person who's not to take out 500. What we do is try to make people happy."

Shawn's passion for handling customer phone calls and e-mails properly has resulted in a very personal approach. "I try to speak or write to people as if it's two friends having a conversation about guitars," Shawn explained. "I don't like phony perkiness, and I don't like that robotic response that almost sounds like voice mail." He does his best to respond to every inquiry the same day. "I believe that everyone deserves an answer."

A customer from Kosovo sent Shawn an e-mail that started with an apology: "I'm sorry for my English," he began. Shawn put him at ease, responding with, "That's all right; you should hear me speak Albanian!" The man's guitar had a broken tuner, and he didn't have a distributor in his country. Shawn got the information he needed from the man, who received the required tuner 10 days later. The customer soon wrote him an e-mail that said, "I used to love PRS guitars and now I love the whole company."

This customer affirmed why Shawn Nuthall is passionate about giving great service. "We have a less than 1 percent return rate. I think we have the best product out there," he noted. "It's easy to support something that is so good. We stand behind the guitars. If there is any problem, we make things right."

PARTNER WITH THE CUSTOMER TO FIND THE BEST SOLUTION

Frank De Fina, vice president of operations/sales, has found that the quickest way to get things on track when dealing with an upset customer is to ask, "What would you like us to do to make things right?" Most customers just want to be heard and understood. Frank has learned that customers often choose a small, inexpensive way to satisfy themselves, whereas if the service provider proposes solutions, they tend to cost the company more money. Seeking a unique solution directly from customers is also a faster way to reestablish good feelings.

Shawn once received an e-mail from a customer who had purchased a rather expensive bass guitar and was having trouble with "string buzz." The e-mail read, "I use a different type of string than you do, and it could be the strings that are causing the problems. I was wondering if you guys would take a look at it." Shawn invited him to send the guitar back to the factory. A couple of days later, the customer asked Shawn to add a feature on the guitar that he hadn't originally ordered. Shawn told him that the work didn't qualify as warranty or repair, but he would talk to the tech and see what they could do. He added that they would have to charge him for the changes. "In the end, we put new strings on it, added the other options, sent it back, and didn't charge him for it," Shawn said. "It technically wasn't a warranty issue, but the guy had spent a lot of money on it, so I wanted to make him happy." It's this kind of passion for great service that has helped PRS grow from a one-man shop to a multimillion-dollar company.

Shawn wants to delight his business-to-business customers, too. Brian Meader, who buys guitars for Chuck Levin's Washington Music Center in Silver Spring, Maryland, carries an inventory of 180 to 200 PRS guitars in his store. Whenever there's a problem, he turns to Shawn to solve it. "Because of how well they make things from the beginning, the number of issues that come up is low. When there is a problem, I have a dedicated person, so I have only a single point contact," Brian said. "Shawn is quick and attentive. He makes it simple and easy. Some manufacturers want to fight us tooth and nail with anything involving a repair. They ask, 'Did you do this? Did you do that? We really don't want to get it back.' PRS understands us enough to know that if we call them, it's serious and not just something we're overlooking.

"There are many manufacturers that say they'll send us a return authorization, but they don't, and we spend a lot of time following up. With PRS, it's never an issue. PRS is known for its incredible craftsmanship and incredible quality control, but if you build enough of anything, you'll find an issue that's beyond your control. If we have an issue with a piece of wood that just isn't right, PRS is always very swift to take care of that stuff. It usually takes me only one contact with customer service."

PRS develops close relationships with its retailer customers. It appreciates the fact that Washington Music Center is a dealer that helps to deflect issues with its customers. It makes minor adjustments and repairs in its own on-site repair shop. "When Brian calls us with a problem, he knows what he's talking about," Shawn said. "I don't question it. I don't pull out my 10 questions. I take it at face value and give him a return authorization."

Brian Meader enjoys a mutually beneficial relationship with PRS. "Because they take such good care of us, we do a ton of business with them, and because we do a ton of business with them, they take really good care of us," he explained. "When I call and say, 'Help me out of a jam,' they pull strings, and I usually get a call in a couple of days saying, 'We pulled this guitar off the line for you,' or 'We changed the color on the order for you,' to help us out."

"We have a very long-standing relationship with PRS Guitars. Paul Smith himself, before he was the famous guitar guy that he is now, used to be a guitar repair guy and did a short stint with Washington Music Center as a repairman. Paul likes to say, 'Before I was a guitar builder, I was the guy who swept floors at their repair shop.'"

PASSION FUELS ENTHUSIASM WITH EMPLOYEES AND CUSTOMERS

Brian Meader has been in the guitar business for several years, and he knows his customers. "PRS is usually the best guitar people will ever own. The average PRS owner owns three of them," he noted. "Our customers like fine things, and PRS guitars are fine things."

Delighting both customers and dealers who sell its guitars is what PRS is all about. "Our products move," Frank said. "The best way to sell them is to hand one to somebody. Some of the world's greatest guitarists are our customers. Carlos Santana, Al Dimeola, Ricky Skaggs, Brad Delson and Mike Shinoda from Linkin Park, and other major artists all play our guitars."

For years, every day at four o'clock in the afternoon, PRS offered factory tours. Enthusiastic employees took turns guiding the groups through the manufacturing process. Because of the emotional connection people have with their guitars, it wasn't uncommon to hear, "Wow, this is where my baby was born." At the time of this writing, the PRS factory is undergoing a major expansion that has temporarily put the tours on hold, but happy customers look forward to seeing them resume.

PRS likes to share its passion with its customers through a semiannual event called "Experience PRS." It's a two-day open house held at the company's Stevensville, Maryland, manufacturing facility. The event allows PRS enthusiasts to enjoy concerts given by celebrity musicians, in addition to guitar-building clinics and factory tours. Every PRS employee takes part in the event. About 1,300 people registered and attended in late 2008. Brian Meader at Washington Music Center brought 200 people. "I would guess they spent a tidy sum to put it on," said Brian. "What other guitar manufacturers do that kind of thing? Nobody."

Customers come to the PRS factory to see more of the guitars they love and to meet all the people who work on them. They also enjoy meeting Paul Reed Smith and mingling with famous artists who play PRS instruments. "Everyone leaves in a total frenzy of 'I've got to buy more of these things,' as our sales attest in the weeks after it. The sales we get from it have been huge," said Brian.

He went on to explain that the guitar-building industry is "an emotional business. It starts with Paul and the culture he's cultivated at the company. Although it's Paul's initials on the headstock, it's the sum of a group of really tight-knit people that makes the company what it is. Much like our store, it's the people who make the company."

"I love guitars," Paul said. "How can I not be passionate about them?" What Paul seeks to create for his customers when they open a PRS guitar case is a take-your-breath-away moment, an "aesthetic arrest," as he calls it. A guitar had just been completed for a famous rock star during Paul's interview for this book. "I want to take it home tonight to show my wife," he said, still excited about each instrument even after more than 25 years running his company. Paul's enthusiasm is contagious. "He's got the energy of a 15-year-old kid. He gets pumped up about a feature or a new stain color," Shawn added. "Everyone comes here because they love guitars. Everyone stays here because they love this company."

PASSION CREATES PRODUCT QUALITY

Producing exquisite craftsmanship and sound quality requires an enormous amount of teamwork from PRS employees. "When you hire people, you can't ask them to love the work they do," Paul explained. "You can ask them to do the job you ask them to do. The truth is, if you're going to get every scratch out of the wood on a guitar when you're sanding it, you can't do that without loving it. It's impossible."

"It's extremely frustrating at times working on a guitar," Shawn added. "Our people need to have a good work ethic." Employees have a love of the craft, a quality that permeates throughout PRS. Inside the pickup cavity of every PRS guitar is the signature of many of the people who worked on it. "My name is probably in 5,000 guitars that I helped to build," said Shawn, who started as a body sander in 2002. "I'm proud that my name is in 5,000 guitars. It also gives accountability, so if something's not right, they can come back and say, 'Hey, what were you thinking when you did this?' No one wants to be the person that drops the ball."

Inspired by the creative way PRS employees bring guitars to life, Frank De Fina said, "There is a piece of the DNA of every employee in the guitars that we sell. Each guitar is the sum total." Paul's passion for dazzling tone quality and tantalizing music inspires a top-down desire to create instruments that are often described by employees as "magical."

It's this passion for guitars and customers that led business-to-business customer Peter Wolf to become sales and marketing director. He was impressed with the company and developed a connected relationship with it. He is one of the few people who now work for the manufacturer who have owned and operated both a retail guitar store and a distribution company.

In January 1986, Peter saw his first PRS guitar. Viewing the United States as the holy land of rock and roll, he flew to the North American Music Manufacturers (NAMM) show in Chicago. There he met Paul and asked if he could be made the exclusive buyer and distributor for Germany, Switzerland, Austria, and Luxembourg. "At first, he sold through me and two other stores in Germany, but after a year, it became clear to him that I was to be the distributor," Peter said. Paul saw Peter's commitment to the PRS brand and gave him the exclusive agreement he sought.

When Peter first began working with PRS, he did so because he ap-

preciated the high quality of the instruments. He also noticed some problems. "The pickups that PRS was using in the late 1980s weren't really
top-notch," he shared. "There were some frequency ranges that they
didn't get right initially. In 1987, my band was touring, and somehow it
didn't sound the way I wanted it to sound. I figured out that it wasn't the
guitar; it was actually the pickups."

Peter talked to Paul about it in 1988. "I was impressed that he didn't
try to talk me out of my perception, He admitted that the pickups weren't
sounding the way they ought to. In April 1989, he switched pickups, and
soon after, more musicians started picking up the guitars. That showed
me that he was willing to listen to people like me." Listening to customers talk about guitars fuels Paul's passion to make constant improvements,
while fueling the loyalty of PRS purchasers.

"The whole brand started to become much more successful," Peter
pointed out. "It showed me that Paul wasn't just interested in numbers;
he was approaching it from a player's point of view. That was something
I thought was worth getting involved with and staying with."

Peter joined PRS Guitars in July of 1997. He now follows Paul's example, making sure that dealers, distributors, and ultimately their consumers are happy and satisfied.

"The more you want to know, the more you'll find out," Peter said.
"When you talk to a buyer or a player, if you break down the barriers and
ask what's important to him, he may tell you things that you wouldn't
find out otherwise.

"We get a lot of praise, but I don't take that too seriously. I want to
hear what we aren't doing well, where our problems are, where we may
not be meeting what the market asks for. I want to hear what the dealers
have to say. How are we doing in the business environment, compara-
tively speaking? Are they able to make enough margin with our products?
Do they have problems with Internet sales? I want to know what they
really think; otherwise I can't help them. What are they asking for that
we may be able to do that we aren't doing right now?"

"We receive e-mails and letters from customers who ask for what they
want. When we get a lot of requests, we pay attention," Frank added.
"We watch markets—the Indie music scene, the country music scene,
and what kind of sounds are making their way into music today—to make
sure our guitars can produce those sounds."

EVERYTHING YOU DO AFFECTS YOUR COMPANY'S BRAND

When asked about his biggest customer service challenge, Peter said, "We don't have one major nut to crack. It's hundreds of little nuts." Whether it's damage control, improving communication, managerial levels, sales, or production, Peter explained, "We are very passionate about what we are doing here, and I try to capture that in our catalogs and make our customers understand that we take every step seriously so that we have a product that is not only competitive but a step above."

"Our product is very well known," Shawn added. "Every move we make is being discussed on the Internet, in magazines, and in print. It's very important that we take care of our customers. They are paramount. We don't build any cheap guitars, so if someone wants to plunk down $500 to $25,000 for a PRS guitar, that's a lot of money. People need to have some follow-up if things go wrong."

Since relationships are valued so highly at PRS, Peter tells employees that everything they do ultimately has an impact on the Paul Reed Smith brand. "Treating our customers with respect and distinction is part of our recipe for being successful. We keep our promises. If you say to a dealer or a distributor, 'This is what I'm going to do,' then you'd better do it," he said, "If you have made a promise to a customer, I expect the company to back you up even if we have to take a financial loss to do it."

FEARLESS PROBLEM SOLVING FUELS CUSTOMER PASSION

Employee mistakes are what Frank calls "tuition toward your education with the company. When I call someone into my office, I say, 'This is what happened as a result of your decision. I'm not telling you that you made an enormous mistake. I think you realize that, and you aren't going to make it again. We're going to chalk this up as tuition.'"

Allowing employees to make customer service decisions in the moment is critical. "People are frequently afraid to make decisions because they're afraid to make mistakes," Frank commented. "When you take that away from the equation, you still get an occasional mistake, but the quality of customer service goes up dramatically."

Frank is masterful at helping employees grow their skills. He came to

PRS in 2008 after 26 years at Panasonic, for 12 of which he served as president of Panasonic System Solutions, a North American branch of the company. He brought with him a passion for providing extreme customer satisfaction, which is in perfect tune with the values of PRS. "To have extreme customer satisfaction, everybody in the organization has to be empowered to take care of customers as if they owned the company," Frank said. "I tell them, 'You don't have to come to me. Just make decisions as if you owned the company and 99 percent of the time you'll make the right decision."

He measures extreme customer satisfaction by "whether people are willing to pay you more for your products." He reminds customer service providers that customers can "fire" the company at any time just by taking their business elsewhere.

When Frank started working at PRS in August 2008, he told his wife, "It's like stepping into heaven." Frank sees a lot of happy employees at PRS. Most of the firm's 265 employees play guitar, which brings a magical element to the company. The instruments are organic in nature, evolving from raw wood. The wood can be unpredictable, and each piece adds something to the unique personality of the guitar. "Our guild of artisans brings the instruments to life," he said. PRS quality standards require that even a minor finish flaw can mean that a guitar never makes it out of the factory to a customer.

THINK OF YOURSELF AS A CUSTOMER SERVICE CHAMPION

Frank summarizes his top three goals as keeping customers at the top of the pyramid, making decisions that delight PRS's customers, and thinking and acting like champions. "When you watch Michael Jordan play basketball, he's magnificent, and it doesn't look like he's struggling at all," he explains. "Champions make it look easy. The cool thing about champions is they don't think about what they can't do. They play at a high level. So the champion salesperson in my mind makes an extra couple of phone calls and does what she says she's going to do. When a client calls and asks for something, think of yourself as a champion customer service person and do what has to be done."

Frank strives to inspire everyone at PRS to become a champion in serving the customer. "You have to get everybody tuned to provide superior customer service. A guitar that's out of tune doesn't sound like an instrument. When you get all the things in line and tuned, it's a wonderful thing."

* * *

Now that you've read the case study for Paul Reed Smith Guitars, consider your own passion for providing exceptional customer satisfaction. Read through the Practical Points, Progress Checklist, and Lessons Learned sections that follow and notice which ideas you are already putting to use in your own business and which ones you can adopt. Then fine-tune your approach to serving your customers.

Practical Points

Point 1: Customer service is about seeing customers as people, not as problems.

It can be challenging to separate the customer from the problem—especially when you're feeling stressed. It's not uncommon to think, "I have a problem on the phone," instead of, "I have a person on the phone." It dehumanizes customers to be viewed as problems, making it more difficult for you to connect with them and to provide a high level of compassionate service. When an unhappy customer tells you his problem, consider asking him what *he* would like you to do to set things right. Customers who feel they are being heard often ask for less than you might think. You can actually create stronger customer relationships by working with them to come up with the best possible solution.

Point 2: Customer service is about making decisions that delight customers.

How often are you on the receiving end of a delightful experience? Is it as often as you'd like? When customers are delighted, they experience a heightened emotional response that stands out in their memories and gets anchored in their minds. Whenever you have a choice of either satisfying a customer or delighting her, take the action that will delight. It can be as simple as having a product ready ahead of schedule or remembering the customer's name. Good feelings are contagious, so prepare to share in the delight and know that the more you delight your customers, the more delightful your job will become.

Point 3: Customer service is about doing what you love to do and doing it well.

Paul Reed Smith said, "You just never know what you're going to love. I love guitars. I love these tools that make music." He also realizes, "You can't force someone to love something." What do you love? You may have a passion for people, or for solving problems, or for the products you're selling. Perhaps you have a passion for making a difference or for taking things from good to great. Paul has a passion for guitars, and by turning his passion into his profession, he spreads his natural enthusiasm to employees and customers. Passion elicits loyalty and support. Good feelings increase when you tap into what it is that you love about your job. This translates into a better, more meaningful experience for your customers.

Point 4: Customer service is about wanting to know what the customer thinks.

The more you want to know, the more you'll find out. The more you know, the easier it will be to provide products and services that best match your customers' desires. Tap into your curiosity and seek out your customers' viewpoints. Customers know what they like and what they don't like. Ask customers what is important to them. When you pay attention to their opinions, you find out things that you otherwise would never know.

Point 5: Customer service is about behaving in a fashion that is consistent with your company's brand.

Everything you say and do on the job, and sometimes even off the job, has an effect on customers' perception of your company. Do you send a consistent message that matches the values and mission of your company? When your service lines up with your company's brand, your customers feel secure and trust grows. Notice what areas of your customer interactions aren't currently matching up to the company's brand and decide how you can better tune in.

Point 6: Customer service is about keeping your promises.

Integrity can make or break a company. That is why PRS backs up its promises, even if the company has to take a financial loss to do so. There are times when you have to make a judgment call and decide on a plan of action. To make the best possible decision, ask yourself what you would do if you owned the company. If you have employees, encourage them to take ownership of situations that arise. If a mistake is made and it costs the company money, consider it tuition toward your education, acknowledge what you learned, and keep your promise to the customer.

Point 7: Customer service is about thinking and acting like champions.

Champions think and act differently from others because they are passion-driven and realize the power of their thoughts. Thinking of yourself as a champion service provider empowers you to take inspired action instead of just going through the motions. You make one more phone call, come up with one more alternative, and stretch your customer service muscles to learn one more skill. Whenever you find yourself thinking, "I can't" or "I don't know how," replace it with, "I can" and "I will find out how." It feels good to be a champion, and it brings about great rewards.

PROGRESS CHECKLIST

As you read the following checklist, rate yourself on a scale from one to ten. Are you applying the lessons learned from the people at Paul Reed Smith Guitars? What can you do today to fuel your passion for your profession and move up a notch in each category?

1-2-3-4-5-6-7-8-9-10

_____ See customers as people, not as problems.
_____ Make decisions that delight customers.
_____ Do what you love to do.
_____ Seek to know what your customers know.
_____ Act in alignment with your company's brand.
_____ Do what you say you're going to do.
_____ Think and act like a champion.

LESSONS LEARNED

The story of Paul Reed Smith Guitars demonstrates how passion can inspire, attract, and retain both customers and employees who love to serve them. To help you ignite passion in your business and your customers, read through the following questions. Answer each one for yourself before reading our responses to start recognizing the champion service provider in you.

1. What can I do to counteract my feelings of impatience with a customer?

   _____
   _____
   _____
   _____
   _____

2. How can I become more conversational with customers?

   _____
   _____
   _____
   _____
   _____

3. Why is it important to create experiences that delight and amaze customers?

   _____
   _____
   _____
   _____
   _____

4. What should I do if I don't feel excited or passionate about anything?

   _____
   _____
   _____
   _____
   _____

5. Is it my goal to get praise and a lot of positive feedback from customers?

   _____
   _____
   _____
   _____

6. How do I recover from a costly mistake?

    _____

    _____

    _____

    _____

    _____

7. Why are employees and customers so affected by a passionate leader
    or coworker?

    _____

    _____

    _____

    _____

    _____

ANSWERS

1. **What can I do to counteract my feelings of impatience with a customer?**

   Shift from being impatient *with* your customer to being impatient for your customer. When you express urgency in resolving a client's issue, the client will sense it and will appreciate your efforts. It's easier to remain calm and focused when you consider a problem as an opportunity to strengthen the client relationship. Impatience is simply an emotional indicator that you need to shift your thinking.

2. **How can I become more conversational with customers?**

   You are more likely to have a relaxed, enjoyable interaction with a customer when you let down your guard. Both a robotic response and fake enthusiasm happen when you forget that you're talking to a human being. Talk to your customer the way you'd talk to a friend and he'll most likely let his guard down as well.

3. **Why is it important to create experiences that delight and amaze customers?**

   Customers have so many choices in today's world. They can research all of their options on the Internet and find an alternative to your business quite easily. Customers stay connected to you when they have a positive emotional experience with you and your product. When you delight them, the connection is even stronger.

4. **What should I do if I don't feel excited or passionate about anything?**

   You can't make yourself feel passionate about anything. What you can do is start noticing what aspects of your life make you feel energized and alive. What makes you wake up with fire in your belly? When you align your career with the activities, products, and people that excite and delight you, your career comes to life. As you go through a typical week at work, notice which aspects of your job bring you the most satisfaction. (If you really aren't sure, you may choose to consult with a professional career coach. There are evaluation tools and materials that can point you in the right direction.) Even if you have to reinvent your position or change careers, tapping into passion in your work life can make a major positive difference in both your work performance and the quality of your life.

5. **Is it my goal to get praise and a lot of positive feedback from customers?**

It's definitely a good sign when positive feedback regarding your products and services flows in. The goal, however, is to give ongoing sustainable value to your customers. To do that, ask your customers what you can do to make their experience even better. Ask for suggestions and ongoing feedback. Peter Wolf says, "The more you want to know, the more you'll find out." Your curiosity and ability to tap into the customer's experience will have her feeling even more committed, both now and well into the future.

6. **How do I recover from a costly mistake?**

The best way to recover from a mistake is to learn from it. Whether you see it as tuition toward your education or as an opportunity to test your integrity by keeping your promises despite financial loss, you will ultimately grow from the experience. Fear of a mistake shouldn't stop you from making decisions. When a mistake happens, do a "postmortem" analysis with your team. Talk through what alternative actions may have been overlooked and what processes could be improved to prevent similar mistakes from happening in the future. Taking immediate responsibility to "fix what's broken" can strengthen the customer relationship.

7. **Why are employees and customers so affected by a passionate leader or coworker?**

People are inspired by passion and the enthusiasm that springs from it. At a visceral level, you can feel the difference when you hear someone talk about something he loves rather than something he simply likes. Passionate leaders will bring out the best in their team. Passion translates into commitment, enthusiasm, and quality. When you're not passionate, you'll know it because you'll feel that "good enough is good enough." When you're passionate, you have an internal drive to perform at the highest levels, and your customers will notice the difference.

WHO'S YOUR GLADYS?

A generally agreeable person can turn into an angry, hard-to-handle customer when he has to deal with a frustrating problem. When you're trying to help an irate customer, do you manage your inner Gladys by staying focused on your passion for service? When a customer has a problem that wasn't caused by your company, would you handle it the way Sean did when he replaced his customer's scratched guitar case without making the customer jump through hoops?

CHAPTER 4

Singapore Airlines: The Tea Service Tells the Story

Singapore Airlines, an international leader of innovation in the skies, flies to more than 66 cities and 35 countries around the world, operating one of the industry's youngest fleets of aircraft. We discovered that it has earned an exemplary reputation, consistently receiving top rankings from prestigious organizations around the world. It has the distinction of having been named one of the world's best airlines 19 times in the past 20 years by one of its industry's notable surveys. It takes a progressive approach to creating spectacular customer experiences by going the extra mile in the areas of innovation and luxury. What really stood out during our interviews with airline Vice President of Public Relations James Boyd was the company's commitment to providing its customers with the highest quality in-flight experience and a heightened sense of personal control. Singapore Airlines knows that being confined in an airplane cabin for as much as 20 hours can turn anyone into a Gladys, so it provides its customers with the best possible service and amenities. In this chapter, you will discover how a room with chairs and a tea service on a table is used during employee selection to ensure that genuinely service-minded people are hired.

Face-to-face customer interactions can be challenging when customers have both feet planted firmly on the ground. Imagine what it takes to keep customers happy when they're trapped in a confined space in-flight for 18 hours or more. Liam Marshall has fond memories of his first flight on Singapore Airlines. A native Australian living in the United States, he and four friends once traveled economy class from Sydney to London.

"It was a fantastic experience," he recalled. "My friends and I took a world trip consisting of eight separate flights, and Singapore Airlines was by far the best." Liam has taken many long-haul flights and was struck by the flight crew's genuine desire to please.

"The cabin crew was obviously well trained," he said. "They had such a great demeanor greeting us." He was surprised to find that even though he was flying economy class, the level of comfort and attention was superb. "It was always okay to push a button in the middle of the night to ask for a drink. That really made a difference to me. They made us feel comfortable."

Liam was also impressed by the well-maintained surroundings. "Everything seemed cleaner and newer than on other airlines, and everything was immaculately presented."

Liam is a frequent long-distance traveler, and this can be quite expensive. He typically buys economy-class tickets. Even in those cases, he noticed, "It could take nearly 20 hours, but when I land, I feel refreshed and comfortable. It's a pleasant way to fly." Singapore Airlines's prices are higher than others, but Liam has always felt that the increased price is well worth it for the enhanced experience.

James Boyd, stationed in New York, knows why customers like Liam keep coming back and selling out flights. "Some of the ways that our flight attendants create those good feelings are obvious," James shared. "They maintain eye contact and use the customer's name." He also points out that many aspects of the airline's customer service aren't so obvious.

"A cup of tea is presented, not served," he explained, "There are subtleties that show that we are focusing on the details." When laying the tray table in first class or business class, the flight attendants always make sure that the logos on the plates are placed at exactly 12 o'clock every time. Every element of the presentation, from where the salt and pepper shakers are placed to the specific way the butter dish is arranged, has been studied and duplicated to create a feeling of luxury and pleasure. Nothing about service delivery is arbitrary, which is why flight attendants spend nearly five months in training, significantly more than the industry average of six weeks. The training focuses on the subtleties and nuances of service delivery, which translates into a high-quality customer experience.

ANTICIPATE THE CUSTOMERS' PREFERENCES

In-flight supervisors observe the flight crew and provide coaching to ensure that the structure of service is followed. They point out what staff members are doing right, encouraging sincere and authentic service. "Giving the crew positive reinforcement is really important, and it's always more effective," James stated. "Customers respond most to service that comes from the heart."

Employees are given the freedom to add their own personality to their delivery. They anticipate what customers want based on personal observations. On a recent trip, James enjoyed watching his flight crew in action. "After observing that a particular passenger selected the garlic bread out of the nine or so varieties of bread that were served, the flight attendant anticipated that preference, and for the next meal, she brought out mainly garlic bread."

Crew members make a habit of remembering whether a passenger prefers red wine rather than white wine with his meal. By observing the customers, they are better prepared to please on the next round of service.

Rebecca Morgan, an international customer service expert, experienced the pleasure of a cabin crew member's focused observation and personality-infused service during a short one-hour flight from Malaysia to Singapore. During the beverage delivery, she struck up a conversation with the lead steward. (Singapore Airlines uses the terms *steward* and *stewardess* to refer to its flight staff.)

She commented on the new uniforms that the airline had just rolled out—dark blue suits with color-coded ties to denote the wearer's status. "He good-naturedly asked how I liked the suits," Rebecca recalled. "I said the stewards always looked sharp." He said, "What about the tie?" Rebecca smiled and told him it looked classy. Sensing her playfulness, he then asked, "And what about my hair?" They both laughed when she said she liked his short-cropped curly hair. The lead steward then offered a fun-filled explanation about why he wished he'd been born with straighter locks.

He left and soon returned; he called Rebecca by name, having taken the time to look her up on the passenger list. "He asked if he could get me anything else, and I jokingly said, 'Chocolate?' knowing that these short flights didn't often have treats like that, and rarely in coach."

A few minutes later, he and a stewardess appeared with a plate of four chocolate cookies on a silver platter. "When I asked if they got them from first class, they said yes," she beamed. "He purloined a treat from another class just to make me happy!"

CATER TO THE CUSTOMER'S NEED FOR CONTROL

Rebecca's short one-hour trip offers quite a contrast to Singapore Airlines's longest commercial nonstop flight, which lasts 18$\frac{1}{2}$ hours. Long flights can take a toll on the mood and disposition of travelers because of the loss of control that is part of airline travel. Passengers must arrive at the airport at a specific time, board at a specific time, remain seated until it is safe to stand, and stay confined inside the plane for the long duration of the flight. In today's high-tech world, the simple fact of being without the use of a cell phone for hours on end can leave customers feeling vulnerable. Singapore Airlines is sensitive to its passengers' need for a greater sense of control and comfort.

There is an instant feeling of comfort upon stepping into one of Singapore Airlines's A380 super-jumbo double-deckers. The A380 is the world's largest aircraft, configured with 400 roomy, economy seats, each with its own television screen. The A380 also boasts the industry's widest business-class seats and first-class suites, complete with double beds and 23-inch flat-screen TVs.

Most airlines easily dismiss the importance of in-flight entertainment systems, considering them a nonessential frill, but they don't have 18$\frac{1}{2}$-hour flights. They don't cover 10,371 miles. "When you're flying for that long, the entertainment system isn't a frill; it is an absolutely critical tool for giving passengers a sense of control over their experience," James said. "When they can start, stop, pause, rewind, and have a broad slate of activities, it gives them a sense of control in an environment where they don't have control."

This psychological perspective is the primary reason that the airline has made a huge investment in in-flight entertainment systems. Passengers control their experience by choosing from over 100 different movies, over 200 video games, and 22 different languages through the Berlitz World Travel Program. The nonstop ultra-long-haul flights have the world's first iPod and iPhone compatibility. "If you want to bring your iPod along, you can plug it into the seat in front of you and watch your videos on the big monitor and listen to your music with a set of active noise cancellation headphones."

The video monitor in the economy class is over 10 inches, larger than the video monitor found in first class on most airlines. "If you're halfway through the rough draft of a document when you run for a plane, you can save your document to a thumb drive and leave your computer at home. We have USB ports built into every seat in business, first class, economy, and suites class. You can plug your thumb drive into the USB port and the 10-inch monitor in front of you, where you usually watch movies, becomes your computer monitor. You can just flip the side of the control unit in the entertainment system and find a BlackBerry-style keyboard. You can finish your document, spreadsheet, or PowerPoint presentation using the entertainment system on the plane."

THE CUSTOMERS' EMOTIONAL RESPONSE REVEALS THEIR DEEPEST DESIRES

Shortly after announcing that it had purchased a fleet of A380s, Singapore Airlines convened focus groups in Sydney, London, Singapore, and New York to get to the heart of its customers' desires. Since the new planes had interiors with 40 percent more space than a typical passenger jet, Singapore Airlines wanted to ensure that it built that space with its customers' needs and desires in mind.

The airline invited its top customers, industry opinion leaders, and representatives from its best agency accounts to these focus groups. James attended the one in New York. The first day consisted of a group outing of cocktails, dinner, and socializing to get everyone acquainted. "The next day, we had a series of activities designed to get them comfortable and get them out of their heads rationally and into an emotional place," James remembers. "We did exercises I will never forget." Teams of participants were formed, and each group was given a set of materials that included construction paper, masking tape, foam core, folding chairs, and string.

On the ballroom floor of a hotel in midtown Manhattan, an area was taped off for each group. "Within this space, using these materials, we want you to create the ideal environment for 10 people for 10 hours," the groups were told. Upon completion, each group presented its creation. "What we weren't looking for was the literal, 'I want the plane to have x.' We were looking for broad themes," James explained. This creative activity—using materials to physically form the airplane interior of their dreams—helped researchers delve deeper into what passengers truly desire. "Psychologists tell us that the level of emotive response is much closer to the passengers' hearts than what they were able to articulate rationally. We were able to really dig into our passengers, not only their psyches but also their hearts, to find out the themes around which this aircraft's interior should be built."

The customers' creations specifically led to the design of the interior of the A380, including the change to a "one-two-one" configuration of seats in each row. It also led to the world's widest business-class seat. "The first-class seats on most airlines have 20 inches between the armrests," James said. "We introduced the business-class seat that was 34 inches between the armrests. We introduced the video monitor in first class that went from 15 inches to 23 inches diagonally. We doubled the amount of in-flight entertainment options. We put a lot of emphasis on the public areas of the aircraft to make it feel more residential, with better paneling and better lighting, softer colors, and more plush carpet that would still adhere to safety standards."

The themes developed by the customer focus groups were reviewed by the necessary experts to determine what was feasible, what would pass the requirements of regulatory bodies, and what was safe in terms of fire safety and weight. An interior design then emerged that held an emotional appeal to customers on the deepest level.

INNOVATION RAISES THE BAR FOR A HIGH-QUALITY CUSTOMER EXPERIENCE

Innovation isn't just a concept at Singapore Airlines; it's an ongoing commitment to provide emotionally enriching experiences. "I've been with the company nine years," James said, "and in that time, we introduced the world's longest-duration flight, the longest-distance flight, the super-jumbo aircraft, and four entertainment systems. There's a real sense of pride in knowing you're offering and operating something that is the envy of the industry."

James Boyd knows that it's not just the down comforters or the private cabins that cause seats to sell out at Singapore Airlines. It's not just about the entertainment system, the attentive crew, or experiencing new and unexpected amenities. It's the way all aspects of the experience come together that communicates an incredible feeling of luxury that resonates with customers.

"I'm proud of the comprehensive nature of this commitment to quality," James shared, referring to the airline's consistent approach to getting things right. It's all based on a commitment to high levels of customer service. "No other airline does what we do in relation to the duration of our flights and the distances we cover. It's important to us to get it right."

To get dining right in an aircraft environment takes a great deal of ingenuity. A galley is not a kitchen. There are no knives, no open flames, and no refrigeration. "It takes about three times the number of steps required to get a meal correct in flight as would be required on the ground. To help us, we enlisted two important panels. One is our international culinary panel of world-renowned celebrated chefs: Georges Blanc of France, Sanjeev Kapoor from India, Sam Leong from China, Matthew Moran from Australia, Yoshihiro Murata from Japan, Alfred Portale from the United States, and Gordon Ramsay from England. Our world gourmet cuisine is enjoyed by passengers in all three classes of travel.

"The panel's talents ensure that passengers enjoy creative, high-quality in-flight cuisine, complemented by an equally illustrious wine selection. It's chosen by our esteemed wine consultants: Karen MacNeil from the United States, who is the chair of the wine program and author of several books on wine; Michael Hill Smith, Australia's first master of wine; and Steven Spurrier from the United Kingdom."

The chefs help create menus and keep Singapore Airlines plugged into food trends from some of the finest dining establishments in the world. They look at the logistics of the food and beverage operation and find ways to provide the kind of meal that customers would enjoy at a five-star restaurant on the ground.

The three wine experts work with a budget of $16.5 million per year to help the airline stay on top of wine trends. They also work in conjunction with the culinary panel to match the right wines with some of the food trends that are translated into actual meals on the aircraft.

"Between these two panels of experts, we are able to reach beyond our area of expertise. We know very well how to make the planes run on time," James asserted, "but these are folks who help us plug into the lifestyle aspects of the flight, which are so important when we have passengers with us for such a long period of time."

UNDERSTANDING CUSTOMER LIFESTYLES MAKES IT EASIER TO SERVE THEM

Various types of customers are attracted to the wide range of high-quality flight experiences offered by Singapore Airlines, three of which are seasoned corporate travelers, leisure travelers, and VFRs (those who are visiting friends and relatives).

"We have a loyal following of corporate clients," James explained. "These are seasoned travelers who live lives that are very different from mine." A couple of weeks after the world's longest-distance flight debuted, James and his staff were shooting media footage on the plane. Afterward, he talked with the passengers. All of them were eager to tell their stories. Many run their businesses in Asia while living in New York with their families. "Because this flight saves me about five hours in total travel time, I'm able to make this journey about three times per month," a happy customer told James. "This gives you an idea of the level of sophistication of our corporate traveler. Many of them fly more than 10,000 miles in each direction three times a month, because they literally live their lives in two hemispheres." Singapore Airlines designs flights to make that lifestyle easier to manage. "For nonstop flights, we charge a 20 percent premium, and we're still selling out most days of the week."

One-stop services tend to attract leisure travelers. They are a little less time-stressed, and they don't necessarily need the saving of five hours of travel time that is offered by the long-haul nonstop flights. Leisure travelers range from value-oriented travelers looking for the best package deal to travelers looking for a business-class seat for their trip to a luxury resort destination.

"We also cater to a number of ethnic travelers from Singapore, China, or Russia who are visiting friends and relatives who are perhaps Indonesian or Malaysian," James said. "They live in the United States, but they have family in Asia. We can count on them like clockwork to travel with us back and forth to their home destination." These customers tend to be main-cabin passengers traveling on their own dime.

Singapore Airlines's customers are typically savvy and very demanding. "They chose us because they are used to the best of everything. They have very specific expectations. Service lapses that would generate a complaint at other airlines generate a huge response at Singapore. It's sort of the double-edged sword of being fortunate enough to earn a good reputation."

Rebecca Morgan provided a customer service session for 90 cabin crew members, whom she described as unflappably gracious. "Their quality of service is so high that it was like teaching customer service to the people at Nordstrom," she said. "In my session, I learned that passengers treat them poorly if there is a problem with the individual entertainment system, or if a passenger doesn't like the food. I can't imagine giving a flight attendant a hard time about these things, but apparently lots of people do." Rebecca learned that despite this harsh treatment, the flight attendants maintain a chipper attitude, happy to fill any request that they can. "Quite a contrast to some of the carriers' flight attendants, who act like they're doing you a favor to serve you half a can of soda," Rebecca added.

STRIVE TO EXCEED EXPECTATIONS

"I feel an unprompted real sense of pride in the middle of a flight to Singapore when I go walking through the aircraft and see how people are enjoying the product, and see the sense of ease they have, and see the fresh flowers—orchids in the lavatories. You see cabin crews scurrying out of the bathrooms after doing their hourly scrub, which I've never seen on another airline. I see a cabin crew member pause for a split second to make sure that the logo on the plate is facing forward when she lays the tray table in front of you at meal time," James shared. "There are a million little things that add up to a consistent message of a quality experience."

In first class or business class, where the crew members have a bit more time, the in-flight supervisor or lead stewardess offers customers impromptu wine tastings. The airline serves nine different wine varietals on board the flight. "This is an experience as removed from the commoditized version of flight as you can possibly be. On one end of the spectrum, you have air travel as a commodity. It is basic transportation that will get you there in one piece. We like to stick to the other side of the continuum, where air travel is an experience."

In response to customer comments, Singapore Airlines redesigned the bathrooms. Passengers in the suites and first-class sections are given Givenchy sleep suits. "Our passengers told us that there is something kind of inelegant about going into the lav to change into their sleep suit and having to sit on a commode," James said. Now, when a passenger walks into the lavatory, there is a leather-upholstered bench that folds up to expose the toilet. "If you'd rather sit to apply makeup or put on your sleep suit, you have a nice comfy bench to sit on instead of sitting on a toilet."

QUALITY SERVICE REQUIRES CREDIBILITY

Why does Singapore Airlines spend millions on wine each year? "It's not so much to give you something delicious in your glass to go with your meal, although that's important," James confided. "The primary reason is to create that point of credible interaction between the passenger and the crew. The taste of the wine is almost secondary. It's the interaction that surrounds the little tiny two-minute ceremony of the presentation of wine that is actually what we are after, because that's what creates the sense of satisfaction for the passenger."

Dom Perignon champagne is served because it's upscale and iconic, but another choice is also offered. Passengers can have Dom or they can have Krug, because the two products have different personalities. "Anyone you try to impress by serving Dom will be even more impressed if they don't have a taste for Dom but more of the Krug sensibility in terms of their palate."

To enhance their credibility, the members of the service staff need a solid base of knowledge, which they gain by participating in ongoing education. The perennial cabin crew favorites include language training and sommelier programs designed to make flight attendants highly conversant with wine. Some trainings are conducted by the wine panel, which is equivalent to getting a master class from the top names in wine in the world.

This ongoing training works so effectively because of the people Singapore Airlines hires. The airline takes a nontraditional approach during early interviews with potential new employees to determine if a candidate has what it takes to succeed at customer service. A group of potential hires is led into a conference room to wait for their interview. There, they find chairs along the walls and a table with a tea service placed in the middle of the room. The room is equipped with a two-way mirror through which the interviewers observe the candidates.

Those who initiate conversations and start to serve others are the only ones who make it to the next round. "It's a way of finding out who has service in their blood," James explained. Those who will, of their own volition, instinctively take steps to look after other people make it to the next round of interviews. They've demonstrated the commitment to service that Singapore Airlines expects of all of its employees.

RECOVERING FROM CRISIS CALLS FOR PERSONAL COMMITMENT

High-quality customer service is never more challenging than when you are dealing with crisis control. While the World Trade Center tragedy was happening on September 11, 2001, Singapore Airlines had two flights arriving in New York, one from Amsterdam into Newark and another from Frankfurt into Kennedy. "I was actually on a plane from Singapore to Los Angeles that made a transit stop in Taipei, which is typically a routine one-hour transit stop," James recalled. "The captain came on the PA system and said that the air space above us had been closed because a pilot had crashed into the World Trade Center. Naturally I thought it was a private plane, and I wondered how they'd repair the trade center. Obviously something very different was happening."

James got off the aircraft at Taipei and activated the crisis plan. The two flights from Amsterdam and Frankfurt were both diverted to Halifax, Nova Scotia, where planes filled the runways. "We had more than 300 passengers on each flight, and there was nowhere for them to go. There were no hotel rooms to be had. There was nothing to rent. They had to come off the aircraft. They had to be fed. They had to sleep. They needed to shower, and they needed communication to get on with their lives."

No one knew when air space was going to reopen. The Singapore Airlines sales staffs in Toronto and Montreal contacted a local high school and found a way to get blankets, cots, pillows, and everything they possibly could to make their customers comfortable. They then created a makeshift dormitory. "For two days, we had all of our passengers living in classrooms, being provided with meals by our local staff members, who had driven, in some cases, hundreds of miles to get to them," James said. "There's no manual for what happened. Our staff members dropped everything and basically devoted themselves to looking after these passengers. It was one of the most remarkable things."

It wasn't just the Singapore Airlines staff members that came out to help. Their entire families came, too. "There's a real sense of ownership in terms of making sure that we do everything we possibly can to look after our passengers."

When things go wrong, service recovery that calms and comforts customers is critical. The first year James moved into the New York office, there was a series of ice storms during the winter. On Valentine's Day, some flights were delayed by more than 36 hours. "At some point, you have to pull passengers out of the planes, find hotel accommodations, and set up transportation. Our office in New York, which has only about 15 people in it, was dispatched to both airports, Newark and Kennedy, and we stayed with the passengers, organized buses, set up meals at the hotels, and gave everyone an amenity pack with a toothbrush and shaving kit."

The Singapore staff kept the travelers informed about the weather, their plane's place in the queue, and projected departure times. "Passengers want to know what you know. They need to know what's going on," James said. Frequent communication proved vital in keeping the customers calm in these unexpected circumstances. The staff then organized the transport back to the airport, getting everyone back on a plane to his destination. Singapore Airlines's staff members stayed customer-focused throughout service recovery, mindful that their customers' lives had been hugely disrupted.

"We need to keep the aircraft on schedule. Delays cost us money and screw up the schedule and everyone's plans. If we give passengers as much info as we have on an ongoing basis, being really transparent and communicating it as we get it, our passengers usually give us a break," James explained.

With a consistent commitment to innovation, quality, and outstanding customer care, Singapore Airlines goes the extra mile to ensure that the passenger experience, even during a crisis, is unparalleled.

*   *   *

Now that you've read the case study for Singapore Airlines, it's time to set your course for delivering the highest levels of customer service. Upgrade your customer service skills to include these first-class behaviors and you will receive consistent high ratings. Read through the Practical Points, Progress Checklist, and Lessons Learned sections that follow and notice which ideas you are already putting to use in your own business and which ones you can adopt. Then set a goal of providing the best quality service to your customers.

PRACTICAL POINTS

Point 1: Customer service is about anticipating customer preferences.

How do you know what your customers want? Your powers of observation can help you provide an extraordinary experience for your patrons. When you notice what selections your customers make or what they express an interest in, you can better anticipate their preferences. If you have returning customers, make a note of their likes and dislikes so that you can provide them with what they want before they ask for it.

Point 2: Customer service is about offering control.

When customers rely on your company to meet their needs, they may experience a loss of power because of this. If customers have to wait on hold or in the lobby of your business, that loss of power can create a feeling of discomfort. If you don't offer the exact product or service they'd prefer, they may feel frustrated by their compromise. The more control you can pass on to your customers, the more powerful and secure they feel.

Point 3: Customer service is about the customer's emotional response.

When Singapore Airlines designed the interior of its A380 super-jumbo double-decker aircraft, it went deeper than simply asking or surveying customers about what they wanted. While those methods would have ferreted out a long list of logical requests, the responses would not have truly come from the customers' emotional centers. To find out what your customers really want, find creative ways to interact with them that allow them to show you. Go out to breakfast or lunch with them and listen for their likes and dislikes. Utilize hands-on customer focus group techniques, and conduct some research beyond a typical written survey. Use that information to produce an experience that will elicit your customers' emotional response. It's the emotional connection that brings customers back to your company.

Sometimes you need to use resources outside of your own to acquire the highest levels of emotional connection with customers. Singapore

Airlines did this by enlisting two panels of world-class experts in food and wine. When it's appropriate, draw on resources outside of your company's expertise to go the extra mile.

Point 4: Customer service is about communicating a consistent message of hospitality.

If you've ever enjoyed a meal at a fine dining establishment, you know the feeling of true hospitality. Your water glass is continually refilled, your every request is met with the utmost courtesy, and you feel like a welcome guest. Communicating a similar feeling in other industries is not as difficult as it might seem. Think of yourself as a personal guide or assistant to your customers as they do business with your company. It's your job to walk them through the proper steps. Make it easy and fast for customers to get their questions answered and their needs met, and they'll return.

Point 5: Customer service is about catering to the customers' lifestyles.

Your customers' lifestyles may be vastly different from your own. Basing service on your own experience and point of view can miss the mark. Take the time to uncover customer lifestyle trends in your industry so that you will be better equipped to aid and enhance your customers' experience.

Point 6: Customer service is about exceeding expectations.

People have come to expect the ordinary. You can make your service extraordinary by tapping into the creativity of the people who work directly with your customers. Brainstorm with coworkers and customers by asking "what if" questions, such as, "What if we were to put orchids in the bathroom?" or "What if we were to follow up every order with a handwritten thank-you card?" By exceeding expectations, you make an emotional connection with customers that keeps them coming back.

Point 7: Customer service is about credibility.

When a service provider doesn't fully understand the products or services she is offering, it can have an adverse effect on the customer's experience with the company. Each point of service offers an opportunity to convey a credible interaction, an opportunity to show your knowledge about your product or service. By striving to gain expertise through ongoing training, you can become an irresistible source that customers come to depend on.

PROGRESS CHECKLIST

As you read the following checklist, rate yourself on a scale from one to ten. Are you applying the lessons learned from Singapore Airlines? What can you do today to take your customer service one step higher in each category?

1-2-3-4-5-6-7-8-9-10

_____ Anticipate customer preferences.

_____ Give customers some control over their experience.

_____ Seek out emotional responses.

_____ Communicate a message of innovation and hospitality.

_____ Cater to customers' lifestyles.

_____ Strive to exceed expectations.

_____ Deliver credible interactions.

LESSONS LEARNED

The story of James Boyd and the people at Singapore Airlines presents a superior service approach that is designed to appeal to the most discerning customers. Consistent attention to comfort and options help customers feel grounded and secure, even during turbulent times. To pick up these innovative skills and make them a part of your everyday practice, read through the following questions. Answer each one for yourself before reading our responses to see how much understanding you've already gained.

1. What can you do to help your customers handle waiting, whether they're on hold or in person at your place of business?

_____

_____

_____

_____

2. Why is it important that you be consistent in the way you present your services to customers?

_____

_____

_____

_____

_____

3. How can you create an innovative approach to customer service at your company?

_____

_____

_____

_____

_____

4. Why should you learn about your customers' unique preferences?

_____

_____

_____

_____

_____

5. Why is it helpful to provide customers with a sense of control over their experience with your company?

_____

_____

_____

_____

_____

6. How can you increase your credibility with your customers?

_____

_____

_____

_____

_____

7. What is the best possible way to communicate with customers during a crisis?

    _____

    _____

    _____

    _____

    _____

ANSWERS

1. **What can you do to help your customers handle waiting, whether they're on hold or in person at your place of business?**

    Customers who are treated to an entertaining experience or an unexpected nicety when they're forced to wait are less inclined to complain about the inconvenience. High-end salons and spas typically offer tea, coffee, or some other beverage to their customers when they're waiting for their stylist or masseuse. Some offer hand massages with one of their scented oil products if there is a long line of customers waiting to check out. And it's always nice when your doctor's office has the latest and greatest monthly magazines in its waiting room, instead of publications from six months ago. These types of creature comforts can soften the impact of the inconvenience of a wait. If a client has to hold on the telephone, waiting for someone to assist her, it can be entertaining to listen to a well-written and even amusing on-hold message.

2. **Why is it important that you be consistent in the way you present your services to customers?**

    When customer service is arbitrary, you get arbitrary results. Plan your service processes, train your employees, and then refine your processes based on customers' responses. Patterns will emerge, and you'll get more repeat business. Document your procedures and processes, then refer to them frequently during staff meetings and in employee communication. Making sure that everyone involved knows exactly what to do will make it much easier to provide consistent, high-quality service.

3. **How can you create an innovative approach to customer service at your company?**

    Creating an innovative approach to customer service doesn't have to require massive expenditures or a lot of labor hours. Don't follow your competitors; lead with new and progressive service ideas. Stay on top of the latest trends through industry magazines and Internet news sites. It may be helpful to visit your competitors' web sites, secret shop their company, or observe the positive experiences you have as a customer of any type of business. Any of these options can give you ideas for enhancing your customers' experiences. You can also begin offering a higher-end packaging option, clearer product training, or more convenient ordering. Watch for processes that can be improved to make things easier and better for your clients, then put forth the effort to evolve those processes to improve them. Your customers will appreciate it.

4. **Why should you learn about your customers' unique preferences?**

    Different types of customers have different priorities. If you have customers who are very price-conscious, you may not want to discuss additional products or services beyond what they originally wanted. However, if other customers are very trend-conscious, striking up a conversation about a new product or technology may be a great way to develop a stronger relationship with them. Asking questions during customer interactions can help you get to know particular customers' unique needs so that you can better serve them.

5. **Why is it helpful to provide customers with a sense of control over their experience with your company?**

    Today's customers know what they want. They are skilled at researching their options, and they often choose to do business with you based on that research. When they have some control over their experience, they feel smart, capable, and calm. It's much easier to be successful with customers who feel good. When customers lack a feeling of control, they can become anxious or even angry, making your job more challenging and the buying experience less satisfying for them.

6. **How can you increase your credibility with your customers?**

    Establishing and maintaining credibility with customers comes from your knowledge and your commitment to excellence. Make sure that you and all of your employees or coworkers are trained and know what they need to know in order to care for the customer properly. If you don't know something, it is perfectly okay to say, "I don't know," although you need to reassure your client that you will get the answer. Always follow up with the answer you promised. Continual education through reading trade magazines, taking classes, and reading blogs can increase your credibility, as you'll know the latest trends and techniques for your industry. Talk about industry developments and brainstorm for new ideas during regular staff meetings and company training. Customers love to work with knowledgeable people who make taking care of their needs look easy.

7.   **What is the best possible way to communicate with customers during a crisis?**

If something has gone wrong, offer your personal apology. Even if the circumstance isn't your fault, you can feel sorry that your customers had to experience difficulty. Going the extra mile to offer a human connection will also help to deescalate problems during damage control. Remember that even when you have no control over a situation, you always have control over your response to it. How you respond will have a vast impact on the results you get with customers. Be as transparent as you can. Tell them the truth. Customers can tell if you are withholding information, and doing so amplifies their tension. Give them up-to-the-minute information and stay in frequent communication.

WHO'S YOUR GLADYS?

How might the mood and disposition of your customers change if they were served by people who genuinely enjoyed working with others? If the members of your service staff were presented with a tea set, would they be inclined to serve others? Would you?

CHAPTER 5

ISCO Industries: A Good Manhole Is Hard to Find

ISCO Industries, a global company, stocks and distributes high-density polyethylene (HDPE) piping products used in various industrial and municipal applications, such as landfills, water drainage systems, golf courses, and manhole installations. The company has a deeply ingrained corporate culture that emphasizes personal relationships, personal integrity, and personal responsibility. When we spoke to the company's visionary president, Jimmy Kirchdorfer, we discovered a leader who is a committed guardian of the quarter-billion-dollar corporation's unique approach to doing business. At ISCO, every employee is empowered by a well-defined mission and a regularly reinforced set of core values. We also spoke with ISCO's regional sales engineer, Chris Ulrich, and its director of customer care, Steve Ramsey, to learn how the company's proactive approach to problem solving results in long-term client relationships. In this chapter, you'll discover what Chris found in the trenches, how his client reacted, and how his personal commitment to excellence came into play.

ISCO Regional Sales Engineer Chris Ulrich was excited when he brought in a large manhole installation job for a major U.S. automotive manufacturer. Or at least, he was until he saw the project specifications. The diagrams had been created by an outside engineering firm, and when Chris reviewed them, he noticed a design flaw. He immediately notified the engineering firm so that it could make corrections. In spite of his efforts, his heads-up was ignored. The manholes were built and sent into the field for installation.

The ISCO team completed its part of the project ahead of schedule.

Then, during pressure testing, problems began. The first manhole leaked. Just as the crew began the repair, the next one failed. One after another, all the manholes leaked. Because of the problems with the original engineering specifications, they couldn't be sealed properly. The project quickly moved to disaster status.

"My client's client was screaming at him, and he was screaming at me," Chris said. He didn't waste any time. He just rolled up his sleeves, put on his steel-toed boots, and spent the next two months in the field fixing the leaks, working side by side with his client in the trenches.

While Chris had field technicians he could have brought in to do the repairs, they would have been billable ISCO staff. He didn't want to create a big expense that wasn't in his client's budget. Even though ISCO had not caused the problem, Chris demonstrated the company's astonishing customer commitment by personally assisting with the repairs at no charge.

"I just went out there to make things right," Chris recalled. He waited until the project was flawlessly complete before providing proof that the original specifications had been faulty and that he had notified the engineering contractor in advance about the problem. The engineering firm was fired, and the ISCO team was recognized as a problem solver.

The repairs took place in the middle of a cold winter and required many late nights. Chris and his client often went out for dinner after a long day of work, so they developed a personal relationship. "I've been to this customer's home in Wisconsin. I've met his mother and father," he said with pride. "This is an example of a contractor who will never use anyone but us, because we solved the problems on that first job at no cost. We helped get his job back on track. He's been to my house several times. We've gone to football games together. I didn't even know him before the job started. That's the type of relationship we develop with customers."

Unexpected levels of personal commitment can pay off in numerous ways, some of which are unexpected. Since this particular job was commissioned by a major corporation, it was written up in several industry magazines read by executives in the landfill and environmental fields. ISCO's responsive approach to solving the project's challenges was called out in the articles. The positive press promoted ISCO's commitment to problem solving, enhancing its image in the eyes of both customers and prospects in its industry.

PERSONAL DEDICATION LEADS TO CREATIVE PROBLEM SOLVING

Chris's strong desire to help his clients is obvious in how hard he works to solve their problems. Rather than throw up his hands when things get tough, he digs in and finds a solution. One year, he had an unusual rush order during ISCO's extended holiday period in December. All the ISCO fabrication shops were on their December break when Chris's biggest client in Ohio received a contract that needed to be completed at a manufacturing facility during a scheduled plant shutdown period. The customer had a short turnaround time to install five manholes. With limited staffing, Chris needed a creative solution that would meet his client's needs.

Because the ISCO CAD department was on holiday, Chris worked with his client directly. They were both at their offices until the early hours of the morning for several days, sending drawings and elevations back and forth until they got it done.

The next step was to solve the fabrication shop dilemma. Chris's local shop was closed, but ISCO had just bought another fabrication company in Florida. Since it was a new acquisition, it didn't yet have the extended December holiday, so Chris moved his customer's order to the southern facility, where it was completed and shipped on deadline.

Even though this client isn't a very demonstrative customer, he sent ISCO's president a glowing letter about the great service Chris had provided and promised to do all his future business with ISCO. Chris was surprised. "It was unexpected, especially from this particular customer. I called him up and said, 'Did you really write this?' He said, 'Man, you did a great job. You really helped us out.'"

Building long-term personal relationships is critical to ISCO's success. As Chris puts it, "If you can get them beyond 'salesperson' or 'contractor' to 'we're both people'—that's where you want to be."

Chris develops his customer relationships by treating each customer the way *that customer* likes to be treated. When he calls up his Ohio customer, there is no laughing and chuckling—it's strictly business. Chris knows what his customer wants, and that's what he gives him. "With some of my customers, there's a lot of socializing and going to football games together," Chris said. "It's all about reading people and knowing what they want."

Chris has clients on both ends of the spectrum. He has caller ID on his office telephone. When he sees a certain number come up, he can anticipate a 20-minute call filled with personal conversation, even if the customer only needs to order a replacement part. While Chris socializes, the other phone lines start clicking in his ear. By the end of the call, he may have several client messages, which he immediately returns.

Fortunately, Chris knows better than to rush the man through their usual informal conversation. "He's a great guy, and he's been a client for years. He gives us a lot of work. He's a customer. For that, I'm happy to talk to the guy for 20 minutes. The message I give myself is, 'This is what he needs, and I can give that to him.'"

It's obvious that Chris feels genuine appreciation for his customers, which is surprising when you consider that he was once pigeonholed as an "engineering type." About two years after Chris was hired, the company brought in a human resources specialist, who administered "personality tests" to determine how each ISCO staff member fit with his position. Chris scored high as a left-brained thinker, someone with strength in organization, logic, and numbers. The high score made sense given his engineering background. However, he scored low as a right-brained thinker, which corresponds to social skills and flexibility. The HR specialist said, "I don't know what you're doing working here in sales. You're not going to be very good at it." She recommended that Chris go back to being an engineer.

The next year, Chris won the title of "salesperson of the year" at ISCO and the HR person moved on to another company. "It's kind of funny because I'm left-brained about details. I still think like an engineer. I don't know where my ability to relate to the customer comes from, but it works."

As an outside salesperson, Chris has many opportunities to cultivate personal relationships with his customers. It's a bit different for inside sales representatives, like ISCO's Todd Miller. They don't have as much opportunity to bond with customers, and they sometimes end up as the scapegoat for issues that aren't their fault. Chris once received a call from an angry customer who was upset with Todd. What had Todd done wrong? Nothing. The customer was seething because his UPS package hadn't shown up. Though Todd wasn't the UPS driver, the customer saw him as the responsible party at ISCO, so he focused his anger on him.

"He knows it's not our fault, but he's upset. He doesn't call me and say, 'Chris, you're an idiot,' because we're friends. It's easier for him to say, 'That Todd!' He just needs a release valve." Chris discussed the situation with Todd, encouraging him to see the customer's anger as just another part of his job. "Let it roll off your back and don't take it personally," he suggested. "He needs to get it out of his system."

Every other year, ISCO cosponsors a getaway to the Caribbean so that Chris and a few of his coworkers can spend time with this customer and his employees. They bring their spouses to enjoy an all-inclusive resort where they can get to know each other as friends. One year, Chris's customer jokingly suggested that he not bring Todd, as the customer's crews would give him a hard time.

The customer explained that when his people go on a job, their profit margin, and the commission that they make on that profit margin, is dependent on how quickly they can complete the project. A few times during his company's relationship with ISCO, some supplies hadn't been shipped or were delayed. This man's contractors were held up and were unable to work for a full day. They had rented equipment that was being charged to their job, yet they couldn't work because the ISCO shipment hadn't arrived. The contractors blamed Todd for their lost wages.

Chris knew that Todd planned on going on the Caribbean trip and that it would give him an opportunity to build his reputation in the eyes of this client and his men. Chris advised him to do some serious socializing. Chris shared, "I thought, 'The next time they're tempted to make an angry call, they might think, "Todd's a great guy! Remember the time we spent with him"'"

Todd took the advice to heart and spent a significant amount of time getting to know the customer's workers and their spouses. While socializing with people he didn't know well was challenging, he saw immediate results when he returned to the job. The payoff? A stronger client relationship.

Chris, Todd, and the rest of ISCO's employees are always aware that customers have choices and could choose to buy from their competitor. Why do they choose ISCO? As Jimmy puts it, 'We want our customers to succeed, and they want us to succeed. It's about long-term relationships."

WHEN IS CUSTOMER SERVICE NOT PERSONAL?

With all of this emphasis on personal relationships, you may wonder, is there ever a time when customer service isn't personal? Actually, there are a few times when staying objective really pays off.

While Chris works to develop friendships with his customers, he never forgets that they are "business friends" and that business comes first. He is careful to let new clients take the lead in determining how personal the friendships become. This can be accomplished by asking questions that let the clients guide the conversation into more personal territory. For example, if you see photos of children in someone's office and the conversation has veered into small talk territory, it's probably safe to ask, "Are those your children?" It's best to stick with lighter subjects and gauge the customer's interest in personal conversation to ensure that the relationship develops at a comfortable pace.

Though a relationship may become more personal as a friendship develops with a customer, when challenges come up, that's when customer service is most definitely *not* personal. Chris is always careful to keep his head when conflict arises. He even has a customer who was a personal friend before he started doing business with ISCO. Now, even when they're out socially, Chris always remembers that his friend is a client. He knows that if he manages his emotions in every interaction with this friend, it will help strengthen his friend's commitment to doing business with ISCO.

Chris continually builds customer loyalty by being thorough, accurate, and responsive. Those three traits create a sense of security for customers. Once they know that they can trust you to look out for their best interests, they come back, even if they stray to a competitor to "test the waters."

It may be disappointing when a customer decides to try a competitor, but don't take it personally. In the end, it can actually be good for the relationship. That's what happened to Chris when a customer confessed that she'd been unable to resist a competitive salesperson's repeated pitch. The distraught customer told Chris the story after learning a tough lesson. "It was only a small order, Chris, so I tried the guy. The order didn't show up, and I couldn't reach him for three days. He won't return my calls, and he's not answering his cell all of a sudden." She apologized to Chris for using his competitor and said, "It was only a $2,000 order. The guy was local. I figured I'd try him out. I learned that I will never use anyone but you again."

Chris did the right thing in this situation by not taking the customer's interest in the other vendor personally. There are many ways to look at the situation, and by identifying with a client's circumstances, a potentially touchy situation can be handled with finesse. Perhaps the client was encouraged by her boss or by the need to make sure that service and pricing were competitive. An overreaction to someone's desire to purchase from another vendor can lessen the chances that she'll come back. Chris's customer had been spoiled by his quick responses and his attention to detail. She was eager to return to ISCO and appreciated it more than ever.

Prompt attention keeps customers happy, which is a lesson that Chris has passed on to several of his coworkers. When a customer leaves a phone message asking for tracking information, another ISCO rep used to feel that he had to have the package tracked before returning the call. Since tracking can take time, sometimes up to four hours would go by before he returned the customer's call. During those hours, the customer would think he was being ignored and get twice as angry.

"You've got to call him immediately," Chris advised him. "Just say, 'I got your message. I'm tracking it, and I'll let you know when I know.' That way the customer can check it off his list. He knows something is being done about it, and he's not walking around wondering what's happening." This proactive approach calms a customer's small frustration before it turns into a big one.

ATTENTION TO DETAIL PAYS OFF

Chris's analytical side pays big dividends with customers. When putting together a quote, he creates what is called a "takeoff," a material list of the pipe and fittings needed to complete that particular project. For each upcoming project, he requests the blueprints and specifications and then builds a list of what is needed to do the job. He then sends this list and his pricing out to the contractors who are bidding the work.

"I break the job down—here's your gas system, here's this, here's that. I include everything the client needs for each segment of the job," Chris said. While his competitors probably go through the same steps, they typically provide only the totals on their bid sheets. It takes a lot longer to quote a job Chris's way, piece by piece, but it's worth the effort. Many customers give him the job because of the way he breaks it down on the takeoff. They often say, "I knew from the way you quoted the job that you understand what I need."

While comparing Chris's quote to a competitor's, one customer said, "This guy's quote lists six valves. I don't know where the valves go. When I look at the ISCO quote, I can see where those valves are being used." The customer for the manhole job actually said, "I get a warm fuzzy feeling every time I look at one of your quotes, Chris. I just know that you haven't missed something big. I know that if I haven't had time to do a takeoff myself, I can take your quote and use it to bid the job. I don't have to worry that I'm going to take a hit on $20,000 worth of material that you missed." Chris's engineering expertise, combined with his attention to detail, gives his customers a secure feeling that keeps them coming back for more.

As companies in the industry that ISCO serves grow, they often hire estimators to ensure the accuracy of their project budgets. Most of the estimators at the companies that Chris calls on now use his bid form, filling in the blanks with what they want and sending it to him. All he has to do is fill in the pricing. When ISCO President Jimmy Kirchdorfer found out about that, he was impressed. "You've got your customers trained to use your quote form and do the takeoff for you!" he said. Chris's direct boss teased him that Jimmy would think he pays him too much for doing so little. Of course, she and Jimmy both realize all the effort it took for him to develop this level of trust with his customers.

Almost all of Chris's customers came to ISCO after he joined the company, and they've all benefited from his hands-on approach. He makes a habit of going beyond the expected level of commitment, even training and certifying his clients to fuse pipe, a process that uses a machine that ISCO sells. The ISCO certification is valued by his customers because it is accepted by state inspectors.

Most of his clients hadn't previously known how to fuse HDPE pipe. Now they do. "I didn't have a clue that by taking all this time up front, I would have loyal customers," Chris shared. "Remember, I scored very low on right-brained thinking. It just made sense to me to go out there."

Chris's personal approach and willingness to offer hands-on assistance are appreciated by his clients. One customer told him, "I had another company come out here, and their guy came out in a suit and tie. I'm not buying from anyone who isn't wearing steel-toed boots."

Chris quite literally put himself in their shoes and got to know them in order to build their trust. Now, he hardly ever goes into the field because his customers and their employees are all trained. Their appreciation for his efforts makes them deeply loyal.

WIN-WIN RELATIONSHIPS BUILD LASTING BUSINESS

One of the reasons Chris loves his job so much is because of the company culture, which places a heavy emphasis on win-win relationships. Customers tell him, "You aren't the lowest price, but I know that if I go with ISCO, what you tell me is what is going to happen, and if it doesn't happen, you're going to make it right. You're not going to disappear from the phone for two days and make me track you down."

What creates that kind of customer trust and confidence? Steve Ramsey, ISCO's director of customer care, explained, "We're successful only if our customers are successful." The people on the sales staff realize that both sides—the customers and ISCO—have to experience long-term benefits from whatever work is done. It's one of the best ways to build mutual trust and respect.

Chris understands that a short-term gain that comes at a customer's expense will backfire every time. He said, "I've never told a customer I could do something just to get a sale." It's this level of personal integrity, coupled with solid knowledge of his industry, that has earned Chris long-term credibility with his customers.

While many buyers in ISCO's industry tend to shop around for the best deal before placing their orders, Chris's customers trust him. It's common to receive a purchase order with an accompanying comment that says, "I'm not going to shop you. I trust you."

"When they do that," Chris said, "I'm going to be extra careful to give them the best price I can, because if they do shop me, I want them to know that I didn't have my hand in the cookie jar."

Chris appreciates his loyal customers and treats them right because they make his job so much easier. He commented, "I don't have to quote them. I don't have to outprice somebody. They are just handing the order to me."

ISCO's focus on gaining long-term customer trust is the result of doing business according to the company's mission statement, which is "to provide long-term opportunities for members of the ISCO team by adding value to our products and services, leading through innovation, proactively executing our vision, and developing mutually successful relationships with our customers."

ISCO's president, Jimmy Kirchdorfer, is straightforward about his customer service priorities. "We put customers first, employees second, and shareholders third," he said. Jimmy believes that the best way to please his shareholders is to focus on making customers happy. The most important thing he wants his employees to understand is that customers have a choice and ISCO has to earn their business. "Even our customers that have been with us forever, we still have to earn their business on a daily basis. That's our responsibility," he said.

There are more than 300 ISCO employees worldwide, with offices in the United States, Canada, and Australia. The company just sold the biggest job in company history in South America. When asked how much of the company's growth can be attributed to customer service, Chris said, "I think all of it is. I really do."

GAIN TRUST WITH PERSONAL COMMITMENT

ISCO's strong commitment to the best possible customer service was firmly in place from the very start. The company originally hired a team of outside sales reps because of Jimmy's strong belief in the value of personal relationships. This makes ISCO stand out among its competition. "I'm competing against computers that spit out numbers all day," Chris explained. "The advantage I have is that I personally go out there and gain the customer's trust. I get out in the field with him and let him know that I'm an expert who can add value to the job."

ISCO's leaders are so committed to this personal approach that it's part of a defined business model on which all growth is based. When new territories are developed, they must have nearby product availability, immediate telephone access, and an expert located within the territory who can meet with customers face to face. ISCO salespeople receive in-depth training, so that they know more about HDPE piping than anyone else in the world. "Anyone can sell pipe, but we add value to it while still being competitive," said Jimmy.

A few years ago, Jimmy, Chris, and Bryan, another sales engineer, met with the president of ISCO's biggest vendor, a manufacturer of the pipe the firm sells. Jimmy was requesting support from the vendor in the form of an exclusive territory. Though Jimmy explained how critical his outside salespeople were for generating business by servicing customers, the vender didn't see the value.

Instead, he said, "You're spending all this money on a sales force, riding around in vehicles, servicing the customers. Maybe you should consider replacing your guys with fax machines like some of your competitors do."

In spite of this challenge, Jimmy was committed to his face-to-face sales approach and sought out other pipe manufacturers. As the company grew, its volume expanded. Soon his original vendor asked Jimmy to bring ISCO's business back to him. Since that time, Jimmy has tripled the size of his outside sales force.

EVERY EMPLOYEE IS AN ENTREPRENEUR

When Chris started working for ISCO in 1997, he was scared. He had never sold anything before. On his first day, he was told, "Treat your area as if it's your own company. We aren't going to babysit you. Here's your truck. Here's your computer. Now go sell."

Chris adjusted to ISCO's entrepreneurial approach quickly. "I love the freedom. It's empowering to be trusted that much and not be micromanaged. In the end, it gives a better result for ISCO. If I were micromanaged, I would feel like my decisions were being second-guessed. That's not the case here. And when I'm successful, it makes me want to go out and sell some more."

At one point, a new estimator was hired and set up in an Ohio office. He called Chris. "There's nobody out here checking on me. What do I do?"

"What did they hire you to do?" Chris asked him.

"They hired me to do takeoffs and quote jobs," he responded.

"Then do that," Chris said.

The new hire was still a bit shaky, but once he got used to the independence, he started to thrive, and now he loves his job.

Everyone at ISCO is vested in the company's success. From the guy who loads the trucks to the woman who answers the phone, all ISCO employees attend the same meetings, have the same goals, and win together or lose together. Each employee is encouraged to think of herself as an entrepreneur, or "a business person," as Jimmy describes it. If you work at ISCO, it doesn't matter if you are a receptionist, a bookkeeper, or a forklift driver; you have the authority to make important decisions on the spot. You have a stake in the success of the company. Providing long-term opportunities for the team is a core value, and that message is constantly reinforced.

This team approach makes every employee aware of the impact he has on customers. Customers expect to hear salespeople say good things about ISCO, but when a forklift driver or a fusion technician or a truck driver speaks well of the company, it captures their attention.

"When customers get a poor impression of you, the damage can last for the next 40 years," Jimmy commented. "We are always going to do what's right in the long term. We don't want people on our staff who intend to get rich quick and get out. We want people who are here to create long-term success. When our people match our culture, it works."

How does ISCO support each employee in becoming the best "businessperson" that she can be? One of Jimmy's managerial strengths is his ability to encourage his employees to discover their own greatness. When it comes to employee development, he explained, "I look at it the same way you do when you're a parent. You want your children to be happy and successful, but you can't make them that way. All you can do is give them the opportunity. You can create a home life so that they have the opportunity to achieve their own dreams. And when they do, you don't take credit for it.

"It's like when Chris Ulrich came to ISCO and had all that success. Our job was just to give him the opportunity. If we hadn't given him the opportunity to succeed, it would have been our fault. When he did have success, it wasn't because of the company; it was because of his efforts."

The company exists to provide long-term opportunities. According to Jimmy, that's why its people are happy to come to work. It's why the company exists. It's much deeper than a paycheck. He wants employees who believe in the company and want to see it succeed.

Once he finds employees who fit the company culture, he keeps them onboard. Sometimes employees find themselves in a job that doesn't fit their strengths or interests. Jimmy keeps people who show promise and moves them to positions that suit them better. He is willing to take someone from the fabrication shop and move her to inside sales. Not everyone's made to be a fabricator or a forklift driver or a sales rep, but if you're a capable person with a great attitude, at ISCO, you can move to another position that will suit you better.

GUARDING THE CORPORATE CULTURE IS ESSENTIAL

With employees scattered around the globe, how does Jimmy make sure that his staff is tuned in to the corporate culture? He acknowledges what works. Communication is critical to achieving both personal and sales goals at ISCO. Everyone keeps current on company news through a monthly newsletter called Florida Flash. Employees are spotlighted for smart business decisions and amazing acts of customer service. High-producing salespeople are featured, as is the driver who got up at two o'clock in the morning on a Sunday to deliver materials to a client by Monday morning. Throughout the newsletter, you see the company's core value phrases—like "long-term opportunities," "win-win relationships," and "commitment." They appear in red text with a yellow flame around it. They aren't just words on a page. They are part of a culture that is constantly being reinforced and embraced by all ISCO employees.

How did Jimmy set up an environment that is so nurturing to his employees? He explained, "I asked myself, 'If I walked into this company and didn't have any ties to it, and I was going to work here, what would I want? What would make me want to jump out of bed and go to work in the morning?' Employees spend so much of their life at work, we might as well make it as exciting and as much fun as possible."

That sense of family is apparent at the company's annual sales meetings. Jimmy knows everybody's name. He knows everyone's spouse's name. He remembers when everyone was hired. Chris was impressed. "I don't know how many people you can find that can walk through a room of employees and know those details," he said. "He even knows their kids. It's crazy. He has a genuine care for employees. He doesn't look at employees as revenue generators. He cares about them as people and wants them to grow."

When asked about this, Jimmy responded, "I don't know why it impresses people so much. I go to a Christmas party and know people's names. It's not hard. We are placing a lot of trust in these people. They are why we are so successful. I should know their names."

Jimmy has a holistic view of ISCO's commitment to its employees. He knows that they work to take care of their families. As the guardian of the corporate culture, Jimmy never loses sight of that. The company's monthly newsletters feature ISCO Kids, and he has created scholarship programs that have helped send employees' children to college.

What happens to employees who don't believe in the ISCO way of doing business? "We get rid of people quickly if they don't fit our culture," Jimmy acknowledged. "One problem with American businesses is that they don't fire poor performers quickly enough. What we find at ISCO is if someone is here for two years, he is usually here for life. But if he is not going to fit our culture, we have to get him 'off the bus.'"

Jimmy believes that talented people with a strong work ethic prefer to work with other talented people with strong work ethics and that people of this type fit the company culture. ISCO is on an upward spiral of growth because its culture attracts these people. He believes that weak people enjoy working with other weak people because it gives them a place to hide their lack of effort or inability. Jimmy depends on employee referrals to fill many job openings, and weak people don't typically get recommendations from ISCO employees. Any weak candidates that slip through are quickly weeded out.

When Jimmy finds high-quality employees who fit the corporate culture, he keeps them. A few years ago, he bought a company but didn't need its sales staff. Instead of letting these people go, he recognized their potential and kept them employed until the right positions opened up for them.

The challenge as the company grows is to cultivate managers who understand the ISCO corporate culture. "Our leaders need to be guardians of the culture. It's the most important thing we do, and we won't do anything to jeopardize it," he said. Right now, Jimmy is excited about the director of international sales, who is in the process of replicating the company culture around the world.

Jimmy gets support in his effort as company president from his brother, Mark Kirchdorfer, the vice president of operations. Mark is also part owner of the company and a strong leader. Jimmy said, "He's a genius at the operations and execution of the company. We have a strong partnership, and I can't imagine the company without him."

Back in 1997, Mark and Jimmy set a vision of growing ISCO to a $100 million corporation. They reached that goal in 2005. To celebrate, they organized a cruise for every employee who was with the company when the goal was set. In 2008 they reached their goal of becoming a $250 million business, and Jimmy personally planned the festivities. He feels that companies don't spend enough time celebrating their success and their employees' efforts. He recognizes how hard his employees work, and he prides himself on acknowledging their success.

To help his staff succeed, Jimmy relies on chief problem solver Steve Ramsey, whose formal title is director of customer care. "Any time Steve hears about an incident or potential situation where a customer could be negatively affected, he proactively calls them," he said. "If anyone in the company finds that a customer is going to be affected because we made a mistake or because a vendor made a mistake or didn't ship something, we want Steve to be notified so that he can call the customer and explain it. He can be proactive to minimize any problems."

Steve encourages ISCO employees to take personal responsibility for problem solving. He writes a customer loyalty column for the company newsletter each month, spotlighting employees who stand out in their efforts. His articles offer perspective-changing advice and examples of employee successes.

In a recent newsletter, he shared his feelings as to how to keep loyal customers by explaining the term *loyalty coefficient*. The article read:

> We know that customer loyalty plays a major role in ISCO's success. It's an especially important focus item for us as our competition increases and the economy struggles.
>
> One method some companies use to gauge their customer loyalty is to estimate or record their loyalty coefficient. This measure is the economic force required to move customers toward the competition. Economic force covers a wide range from price and availability to service and support.
>
> As you know, we do many things every day to continue to earn our customer's loyalty. I'll only point out one here from June.

Steve continued with an example of how Bruce, an inside salesperson, demonstrated a personal commitment to getting a rush order delivered on time. Bruce got notice of a large order late one afternoon that had to be delivered the next day. Handling the request took great effort by a few ISCO employees. First, the Riverport shipping team quickly boxed 60 eight-inch fittings and convinced the FedEx Freight driver to wait for them to finish before leaving. Then, in Houston, despite being shorthanded, the shipping team boxed the order in the early evening, and it was delivered to a FedEx/Kinko's drop site just five minutes before the air shipment deadline. The customer was ecstatic, and Bruce attributes the increased business they've seen this year to that kind of service.

Steve walks his talk by attending to his customers' loyalty coefficient in every aspect of his job, including the message on his answering machine. Customers know they are going to get a quick return call when they hear the words, "I am continually checking my messages throughout the day."

Customer opinions help Steve gauge and make adjustments to provide better service. He sends survey requests out with shipments to measure customers' loyalty index. The most important question is, "Regarding your recent work with us, how likely are you to recommend us on a scale of 0 to 10?" ISCO consistently gets high marks.

Before Steve came to ISCO, he worked for an airline carrier. "It was a great training ground," he said. With canceled flights and changing schedules, Steve had ongoing opportunities to work with angry customers, so he quickly learned how to manage his emotions and focus his energy on the customers' needs.

When a customer is so angry that you feel as if you're under attack, Steve suggests that, "Instead of getting defensive, get into their shoes. Immediately show that you are on their side. Don't just say it—back it up."

From his airline experience, Steve learned not to take it personally when things go wrong, even if he had made the mistake that led to the problem. When customers are yelling and screaming at you, Steve suggests four responses that can smooth things over quickly: show compassion, become their advocate, demonstrate concern, and focus on creative solutions.

CREATIVE SOLUTIONS MAKE CUSTOMERS FEEL SECURE

What do you do when a customer needs your product, but you have a shortage of supplies? Steve's skills in customer care are most evident when things go wrong. For a large customer project, he knew that waiting for back-ordered fittings would delay the customer's job, so he immediately researched other options. He crafted a design that allowed him to replace the back-ordered fittings with another type that was in stock. Once his customer confirmed that the design would work, Steve shipped the substituted parts overnight to ISCO's Florida fabrication shop, where they were customized to create an outlet that would function perfectly to his customer's specifications. Steve literally invented a solution that was manufactured and delivered to the customer in record time.

Steve sidestepped another potential customer service problem by focusing on just-in-time delivery of the parts. A customer ordered 200 fittings, but Steve's supplier didn't have enough stock to send them all at once. "Right now, what do you really need?" he asked his customer. That "right now" focus helped him find a realistic, workable solution. He talked to the customer about how many fittings its people could install per day. With that more realistic number, Steve got to work to produce a four-day supply. He had two men work late into the night to make 80 fittings and drive them directly to the job site. Then Steve laid out a schedule to get the fittings to the customer "as needed." It was an example of ISCO's commitment to creative problem solving and great customer service in action.

How does ISCO ensure that its staff is in the proper mindset for providing the best customer service? Continuous learning and improvement is a core value of the company. Employees are encouraged to stay at the top of their game in professional and personal development. Even people who only answer phones on occasion are encouraged to take customer service training.

Jimmy trusts employees to decide for themselves what type of training they need. To encourage commitment, employees pay a percentage of the cost of any courses they choose. "If I spend $2,000 to go off to a workshop somewhere, it's going to cost me about $300 out of my pocket. It's not a lot, but it's still something, so there is some accountability," explained Chris Ulrich.

Chris has taken Dale Carnegie courses and participated in some Franklin Covey training. He hasn't had a training expense questioned in 10 years. Jimmy told Chris, "If the value you're getting out of it is worth the cost, then I'm going to trust your judgment."

The most transformational training that Jimmy makes available to his people is a personal development program taught by the Hoffman Institute in Napa Valley, California. The training is focused on personal growth rather than business skills. ISCO recognizes that personal skills inevitably translate into professional success. More than 70,000 people worldwide have used the Hoffman training to achieve greater life balance and overall well-being. It's an intense eight-day training program and a big financial commitment. After Jimmy took the training, he saw the value of unlearning old patterns and acquiring tools to improve his overall quality of life. He now offers this training as a gift to those employees who he believes would most benefit from it.

Unlike the other educational opportunities that are made available, Jimmy personally picks the people who get to go through the Hoffman process. Chris was the seventh person to be selected. It's not just top-line management or top salespeople who are offered the gift. Jimmy has sent an administrative assistant, an accounts receivable specialist, the human resources manager, and a purchasing agent.

When Chris Ulrich attended the training, he didn't know what to expect. One of the attendees at Hoffman asked, "What the heck are you doing here? Shouldn't you be at a sales training this week?" Chris didn't know what to say until he had completed the course. He came back with tools that made him a better husband and a better father to his two sets of twins. But did it make him a better employee?

"After going to Hoffman, I've definitely changed my reaction when things go wrong," Chris said. His coworker Todd noticed the change immediately. A few weeks after Chris got back from the training, he said, "Chris, you're so calm!"

Chris asked Jimmy what he gained from sending his people to the program. Jimmy replied, "I've been through the program myself, and I know what it did for me. I've seen it transform people's lives. It's a great gift to give to those who have demonstrated a commitment to self-improvement. Giving our people the gift of these tools to make them more successful and happy in their personal lives will also make a difference in their business life. People will be more likely to help each other. If problems arise, they can easily put things in perspective. It's giving a gift. That's the benefit I get out of it."

Chris noticed the change in himself right away. "I became so much better a husband and father. I have the tools to be more present with people in my personal and professional life. I know it's not my fault when the UPS guy doesn't show up. There's nothing I can do about it," he noted. "If the customer wants to yell at me, I let him yell at me. I used to call Todd and yell at him about it. Todd can't do anything about it, either. I learned that if there's nothing I can do about it, I'm not going to get upset, and if there is something I can do about it, then I'm going to take care of it right away. I'm not going to put it off and let it grow into something bigger."

*   *   *

Now that you've read the case study for ISCO Industries, it's time to think about how you can develop your personal commitment to delivering exceptional customer service. Read through the Practical Points, Progress Checklist, and Lessons Learned sections that follow and notice which ideas you are already putting to use in your own business and which ones you can adopt. Then set a personal goal for bringing your company's mission and core values to life.

PRACTICAL POINTS

Point 1: Customer service is about long-term thinking.

When you're busy, it's tempting to take the quickest course of action instead of making the extra effort to truly serve the customer. In most cases, the small effort that is required to make customers' lives easier pays off in long-term loyalty. It pays to remember that a customer's loyalty is earned, not given. When Chris demonstrated his personal commitment to the client by working without pay to get the job done, he earned loyalty and years of additional sales from that client.

Point 2: Customer service is about win-win relationships.

The best kind of negotiation is the kind where both your customer and your company come out ahead. A win for a customer can be anything from feeling respected to getting a job done on time and under budget. A win for your company could be giving the customer a credit for its next visit instead of providing a cash refund or holding the line on pricing when you know your product's value. Win-lose relationships can have devastating long-term results. Make a habit of creating opportunities for both your company and your customer to win. Your efforts will create the kind of trust that makes it easier for customers to do business with you instead of your competition.

Point 3: Customer service is entrepreneurial, regardless of your job description.

Viewing your job as your own business can lead to outstanding results. Take personal responsibility for making sure that everything within your realm of responsibility runs smoothly. Look at what can be improved, and then take action to make it better. When your department is functioning flawlessly, you can't help but deliver better service to both your internal and your external customers.

Point 4: Customer service is about putting the customer first.

Every day, you're faced with assignments, challenges, and responsibilities. Sometimes a customer walks through the door or calls on the phone while you are preoccupied with other things. When in doubt, always put customers first. Greet them warmly and give them your full attention. Answer their questions directly or let them know that you are getting the appropriate person to help them right away. When customers feel important, they stick around.

Point 5: Customer service is about creative problem solving.

Every dilemma has at least three or four possible solutions, though there may be downsides to some of them. When customers know that you're committed to solving any issues that arise, you become a customer's first and best choice. One way to ensure that you're being creative is to come up with at least three possible solutions to every problem, even if the last one is a bit ridiculous. You may be surprised by the creative answers you uncover.

Point 6: Customer service is about personalizing your approach.

Customers come in a variety of styles and personalities. Some are chatty, while others prefer to get to the point and move on. Instead of treating customers the way you'd like to be treated, take it one step further and treat them the way you think *they'd* like to be treated. If they are method-ical, break things down into steps. If they are big-picture thinkers, give them the overview. Pay attention to your clients' body language so that you can predict their moods and emotions more accurately. By personal-izing your service to the unique needs of each customer, you will develop relationships that last.

Point 7: Customer service is about asking useful questions.

Sometimes a customer service situation is so challenging that you may not see a solution in sight. By asking yourself and your customer some useful questions, you move in a positive direction and get back on track. To get into the right frame of mind, ISCO's director of customer care, Steve Ramsey, asks himself, "What is the best scenario?" Then he consid-ers these key questions: "Right now, what will help? What do you really need? What is realistic?" By separating absolute necessities from what are simply "wants" in any given situation, you're more likely to come up with a workable solution.

PROGRESS CHECKLIST

As you read the following checklist, rate yourself on a scale from one to ten. How well are you applying the lessons learned from the ISCO team? What can you do today to bump up your scores in each category?

1-2-3-4-5-6-7-8-9-10

_____ Use long-term thinking.

_____ Develop win-win relationships.

_____ Think like an entrepreneur, regardless of your job description.

_____ Put your customers first.

_____ Be a creative problem solver.

_____ Treat customers the way they want to be treated.

_____ Ask useful questions.

LESSONS LEARNED

The story of Jimmy Kirchdorfer and ISCO Industries presents a variety of skills for creating a personal approach to everyday customer service situations. To help you extract these skills for yourself so that you will gain long-term rewards, read through the following questions. Answer each one for yourself before reading our responses to see how many creative ideas you can generate.

1. What does personal growth have to do with customer service?

    _____

    _____

    _____

    _____

    _____

2. What do company goals have to do with customer service?

    _____

    _____

    _____

    _____

    _____

3. How do you keep a customer service culture alive?

    _____

    _____

    _____

    _____

    _____

4.   What is the best way to minimize conflict in client relationships?

_____

_____

_____

_____

_____

5.   What can set you apart from your competitors, making them virtually irrelevant?

_____

_____

_____

_____

_____

6.   How does considering yourself an entrepreneur make a difference in customer service?

_____

_____

_____

_____

_____

7.   What's the most important thing to remember about your loyal customers?

_____

_____

_____

_____

_____

ANSWERS

1. **What does personal growth have to do with customer service?**

    To grow in your position or in your career, you will have to grow and mature personally. Taking action to improve yourself and your customer service skills will help you in many ways. You will feel more grounded and better able to cope with changing times. It's ironic, but the more you learn, the more you find that there is to learn. Lifelong learners stay at the top of their game and have greater ease in handling the unexpected.

2. **What do company goals have to do with customer service?**

    When a customer has a great experience, she is more likely to tell her friends, family, and work associates about your company. Plus, it is significantly more difficult to get a new customer than it is to keep an existing customer. Your contributions in customer service help your company reach and exceed its sales goals. And when a company is successful, this could translate into a better workplace environment, higher pay, or career growth for you.

3. **How do you keep a customer service culture alive?**

    Our research has taught us that companies that acknowledge their employees, explain and reinforce their core values and mission, and communicate with their staff members on an ongoing basis have the strongest customer service. Great companies define their corporate values and beliefs. They convey these to their employees using a variety of media, including meetings, e-mails, and print materials. Employees keep the culture alive by relying on the company's core values to guide their customer service interactions.

4. **What is the best way to minimize conflict in client relationships?**

    Personalize the relationship. When a client sees you as a likable person rather than as just a representative of the company, you get more cooperation and less blame when things go wrong. Once urgent business is complete, take the time to ask a question that might lead to a more personal conversation. Questions like "Do you live far from your office?" or "Have you been with your company for long?" can turn a conversation in a more personal, relationship-building direction. Be careful not to get too personal too quickly, though. Once you've established a business friendship, most customers want to see you succeed and are more likely to ask for your help when they need it.

5. **What can set you apart from your competitors, making them virtually irrelevant?**

    Your personal commitment to creating the best possible outcome in every challenging situation will make you stand out from your competitors. Many businesspeople shy away from conflict or extra effort, particularly when something goes wrong. When you remain calm and resourceful during challenging times, you are in a better position to add value to the customer's experience. If you go into any adverse situation with a strong commitment to finding a workable solution, then don't stop until you find it, you will be rewarded with client loyalty and inevitable success.

6. **How does considering yourself an entrepreneur make a difference in customer service?**

    People who own their own business have to take personal responsibility for every aspect of their success. Translated into a corporate atmosphere, you can consider your personal area of the business to be your complete responsibility. If something is not functioning properly, take the responsibility for making sure that it gets fixed. If other departments aren't providing you with what you need to do your job, take the responsibility for working with them to resolve the issue. While it's easy to let things go and think, "That's someone else's job," the extra effort will translate into success in many areas, including customer service.

7. **What's the most important thing to remember about your loyal customers?**

    Business is competitive, and even your most loyal customers always have a choice about where to take their business. Don't take them for granted. There is a large number of economic forces, including price, product availability, service, and support, any of which might influence customers to consider the competition. If you take the approach of "earning" your customers' business every day and treating them well, they're less likely to try someone else.

WHO'S YOUR GLADYS?

You may encounter a screaming client who is under incredible pressure from his own screaming customer. Will you take it personally, or will you take personal responsibility for setting things right, the way Chris handled the manhole cover disaster?

CHAPTER 6

The Green Company: Who's Going Up the Ladder?

The Green Company, a nationally acclaimed residential building business, creates "lifestyle communities" for home buyers. Building homes and developing new subdivisions is its business, although its purpose is to create neighborhoods that appeal to empty nesters and retirees in New England. Founded in 1953 in Plymouth, Massachusetts, it was the first company to win three of the home-building industry's most coveted awards in the same year. Founder Alan Green has been inducted into the Builder Hall of Fame. We discovered that even during turbulent economic times, the Green Company remains sound as a result of its excellent reputation. What really stood out during our interviews with CEO David Caligaris and members of his staff were the lengths to which the company will go to support and educate its customers. From the beginning of the customer relationship to long after the warranty period has ended, home buyers are treated with respect, care, and concern. By establishing a long-term perspective, the Green Company has been able to sustain ongoing referral business, even during downturns in the building industry. It will warm your heart to discover how one of the Green Company's employees handled a panicked elderly couple with a problem that was out of reach.

Though well into his eighties, Alan Green, founder of the Green Company, is still actively involved as chairman of the company. He makes a personal phone call to every buyer who reserves a home. He continues to walk every foot of the properties where new developments are to be built. His enthusiasm for long-term customer relationships has endeared him to home buyers and inspired his employees to take a long-term approach to service.

"Alan always takes pride in everything he does," said Customer Care Manager Lois MacIsaac. "He will do anything, including sweeping the floor. Nothing is beneath him. He taught us to do what needs to be done."

According to the company's sales department, what needs to be done from the first point of contact is to make customers feel welcome and comfortable. At a Green Company model, Sales Director Rebecca Geary told us, "Our low-key, casual approach puts everyone at ease. We get frequent comments on visitor surveys from people who were expecting higher sales pressure. They tell us how pleasant it was to come in and be left to their own devices to wander through the models."

Salespeople are accessible, while still allowing visitors breathing room to explore the homes on their own. While they walk through the houses, delicious cookies and refreshments are provided to create a more pleasurable experience.

FOCUS ON THE BENEFITS OF WHAT YOU HAVE TO OFFER

The Green Company satisfies customers by focusing on their dreams. As it says on its web site, "We create entire communities of distinction and enduring quality . . . places you'll be proud to call 'home.'"

"We sell more than just a house. We sell a lifestyle and a community," noted David Caligaris. Typical buyers are empty nesters, in preretirement or retired. Their children are grown, and their circle of friends, which had once been closely affiliated with their offspring, has narrowed. "They're looking for a new start. The lifestyle we offer is the biggest factor for them."

A typical Green Company community consists of 400 to 550 homes, built with strict emphasis on the land's natural features. Many include golf courses or waterfront recreation areas. All the developments have pools and clubhouse amenities to encourage neighbors to socialize.

"In one development, we're trying a community store and post office where everybody will come to pick up mail each day," David explained. "There are chairs, café tables, and a cozy feeling. It's a place where people can grab their mail, chat, and have a cup of coffee."

Green Company representatives go into their newest neighborhoods once a month, inviting everyone to a Saturday morning coffee. They are there to encourage homeowner relationships. They assist the community by setting up events and bringing in experts to create special-interest groups within the community. One example is the bridge instructor who taught homeowners how to play the popular card game so that the community could form a bridge club. They also facilitate quarterly breakfasts, art shows, and garden tours to create opportunities for homeowners to interact. This attention to the long-term happiness of their communities keeps the Green Company's reputation strong among homeowners.

David believes that customer service in his industry breaks down into two pieces: the building experience and the community experience. "Once you address both of those pieces, our buyers want all of their friends to come. Happy customers are our best salespeople." Prospective home buyers are often invited to neighborhood events, so that they hear about the neighborhood's assets from current residents.

MANAGING EXPECTATIONS KEEPS CUSTOMERS CALM

Anyone who has ever bought a new home and then watched as it was built can attest to how challenging this can be. A home is a major purchase, and the process isn't always smooth or pretty. One of the ways in which the Green Company has earned a better than 50 percent referral rate is through its management of customer expectations. To minimize stress during the building process, the company always tells new customers everything—the good, the bad, and the ugly—that they will encounter during the buying and building process. David Caligaris believes that this is critical for keeping customers calm.

"They are watching every step of the way. They see their home in its early ugly stages and its later beautiful stages," he noted. "At one point, they'll walk into the house, and there will be water in the basement. It's not yet weather tight, and water will get in, but it's not a problem." If they don't understand the normal phases of the building process, customers can become alarmed.

"Up front, we explain what they will experience. We try to tell them all the unpleasant things, so that when those things happen, they remember and have a frame of reference."

At every stage of the process, the Green Company keeps in close communication, offering buyers a contact person to talk to when they see something that bothers them. Anticipating customer reactions and being available is instrumental in sidestepping some of the stresses of home building.

"We set the right expectation," Sales and Marketing Vice President Dominique Sampson added. "When you buy a shiny new car, it looks good and it works perfectly. When you buy a house, customers get hit with big-time buyer's remorse because they spend a lot of money on something they won't see for eight to ten months. We spend a significant amount of time maintaining that relationship. We analyzed our points of contact and realized that we are in touch with buyers one way or another more than 40 times, with meetings, appointments, invitations to events, and letters with photos of their property."

In an industry that is notorious for extending completion dates, the Green Company goes to great lengths to satisfy the customer's delivery expectations. "If we say you're going to close on June 1, then we'll have your home ready on June 1," Dominique said, proud that the company has developed well-scheduled construction timetables. "Delivery dates are sometimes moving targets, although 99 percent of our homes close on or before our target closing dates."

CUSTOMER PERCEPTIONS MATTER MORE THAN THE TRUTH

Managing expectations and ongoing customer satisfaction is part of the Green Company's culture. "We have to have a long-term perspective," David Caligaris explained. "We need to ensure that our existing customers are satisfied. It could be 10 years down the road when a friend of theirs is looking for a place to retire. We want them to recommend us."

Dominique knows that customers feel good about endorsing the Green Company. "Customer surveys show that over 95 percent of our homeowners say they would recommend us to friends or relatives."

The closing, the contract-signing meeting during which ownership of a new home is officially turned over to the home buyer, is a critical time for managing customer perceptions. The Green Company's goal is not only to deliver the home 100 percent complete at that time, but also to make sure that the customer agrees that it is 100 percent complete. Its employees know that the customer's perception can be far different from the company's, so the communication that occurs at closing is critical. "We need to know what the customer thinks," David said. "As soon as we started asking the customers to give us their perception, we found that it was different from ours. Their perspective is all that matters in how they talk about you to other people."

Home buyers typically see a warranty issue that comes up at the closing as a failure to complete the house. "You can get them to sign off on it, but they get nervous. Instead, we do a walkthrough a few days ahead of time. We then make sure they come back through a half-hour before closing, so they know that we fixed all the issues. That gets them to a psychological perception that it is complete. The next problem that comes up is then a warranty item."

TEAM MEETINGS KEEP EVERYONE FOCUSED

The Green Company supports its strong customer service effort with mandatory meetings every Tuesday morning. Twenty employees from various departments gather together. "We mine our notes so that everyone knows what's going on with every customer, from the first visit through the last," Dominique shared. They may discuss what's happening with customers even three years after they've purchased a Green Company home. Hearing about the happenings in different areas within the company helps employees develop compassion for the unique challenges faced by other departments and reinforces teamwork.

The meetings also help employees at the lowest level in the organization embrace the company culture. They hear how senior-level managers handle difficult situations, so they gain the confidence to take the initiative when something goes wrong. "It's what people hear in that meeting—how we deal with more delicate issues and how we react—that helps them figure out how to deal with the smaller issues they come across," David explained. "Once you get that in place culturally, you get everyone in the right mindset."

The weekly meeting is also instrumental in keeping each customer's needs in the forefront of everyone's mind. The employees get to know and like their customers. "Buyers follow us from one development to another," Rebecca said. "They hug their coordinators. It's interesting to see how often they develop relationships that are long-term." She pointed out that a happy customer won't necessarily stay satisfied without ongoing attention: "It's important to remember that customers are always asking 'What have you done for me lately?'"

FIND WAYS TO SERVE AFTER THE PURCHASE

Rebecca Geary once received a call from a homeowner who could not find the plans for a few condos she had purchased in the 1970s. "I found the plans and sent them to her," Rebecca recalled. She enjoys helping customers long after the home is built and warranty period is over. She knows how critical it is to nurture lasting relationships, since it's what gets future referrals.

A significant way in which the Green Company takes a long-term approach is through its Customer Care Department, which was created to tend to customers after they move into their homes. The customer care team handles warranty work and what the Green Company calls "Residential Services," an area that was created to manage homeowner repairs and maintenance after warranty expiration. For a nominal hourly rate, the team helps homeowners with basic tasks and advice. It's an area of the company that is not highly profitable financially, although it supports the company's long-term approach and helps to bring in referrals. "If you need someone to help you out, it's hard to get the jack-of-all-trades to your house," David explained. "Residential Services can send one of our guys to hang pictures, hang drapes, put in a door, or even finish a basement. It helps with the whole lifestyle. In terms of the physical building, it gives us a way to tell the homeowner that her house is out of warranty, but we can still help her. It's a way of softening the no."

There are times when Lois MacIsaac chooses not to charge a homeowner at all, in the interest of enhancing the relationship. "I had a woman whose husband passed away. She called wanting to know how to change the furnace filter, turn off the outside water for the winter, and other basic home maintenance tasks," Lois recalled. She was happy to spend an hour with the homeowner, going over the home-care basics, without charging her. "It's what I would have wanted someone to do for me."

Lois felt that same pang of compassion when an elderly couple called in a panic. "Our smoke detector keeps going off," they said. Lois started to give them suggestions, then thought better of it, "I didn't want them climbing up on a ladder," she explained, choosing to visit their home herself to check on the situation. Instead of a smoke detector, Lois discovered a chirping plug-in carbon monoxide detector that was low on battery power. Even though it was neither a product supplied by the Green Company nor a home warranty issue, Lois was happy to have solved the mystery for the nice couple and to replace the battery at no charge.

DO THE RIGHT THING FOR DIFFICULT CUSTOMERS AND DIFFICULT SITUATIONS

It feels good to help out friendly people, but sometimes the people who call the Customer Care Department at the Green Company have abrasive personalities. Some can be downright insulting. One such woman called Lois with a ceiling problem. Lois kept her emotions in check and called her boss. "I told him that just because she was insulting doesn't mean we shouldn't look at it." They sent someone out and determined that a repair was in order. Lois told the woman, "We will work with the drywall people and tell them not to charge you for repairing the ceiling." She also had some bad news, informing the homeowner that the firm could not repair the custom paint on the ceiling, as the warranty covers only a standard paint finish.

"She was upset in the beginning," Lois shared, "but I have found that when you have bad news, give it as calmly and directly as you can." Developing the skill of remaining cool-headed with customers has served Lois well. In the end, the repair was made to the customer's satisfaction. By treating abrasive clients with the same respect it gives to pleasant patrons, the Green Company maintains lasting relationships. When asked what customer service means to her, Lois said, "Follow up and follow through. Even if I have bad news, I want to call them and let them know. Communication is key."

While Lois realizes that she can't give customers the exact answer they are looking for every time, she always listens. "Once, a homeowner called and said, 'It's really cold in my bathroom,'" she recalled. "The house was out of warranty by two or three years. I immediately thought that we shouldn't get involved. But you always owe them a conversation.

"As it turns out, this homeowner's heat duct had been installed under the bathroom vanity. It was our fault. I learned a lesson about really listening, even when I thought I was right."

The Green Company's commitment to doing the right thing is also prevalent among its employees and vendors. David Caligaris recalls an unfortunate incident in which a customer, after completing a walk-through, found that her wallet had been stolen. Fortunately, the building crew working on-site shared the company's concern for the customer. "Our two construction guys emptied the whole dumpster piece by piece," David shared. "It took three hours sifting through a lot of junk. They found her wallet and credit cards. They didn't find the money, but the customer saw that these people really cared and went all out to find where the wallet was tossed.

"They ultimately figured out that the culprit was associated with an-other vendor. We were grateful that the vendor made restitution. The guys couldn't do enough to try to make up for the bad experience. It was an unfortunate thing that happened, but what our construction guys emphasized to the customer is that we really care. I was struck by that."

Doing the right thing results in long-term relationships, which is vital when facing a downturn in the economy. "All builders are subject to changes in the market," David said. "We've been through several cy-cles over the last 50 years. We're one of the last builders to slow down and one of the first to pick up. We always have a list of people who want to buy from us; they just have to sell their house first." Dominique was quick to add, "Our volume may go up and down, but our goals are always the same: to help our customers realize their dreams through their home."

* * *

After reading the case study for the Green Company, what ideas will you take away? Read through the Practical Points, Progress Checklist, and Lessons Learned sections that follow and notice which ideas you are al-ready putting to use in your own business and which ones you can adopt. Then set a goal for improving your long-term approach to serving cus-tomers.

PRACTICAL POINTS

Point 1: Customer service is about offering a low-pressure, high-pleasure experience.

Today's customers have a low tolerance for high-pressure sales. Create a welcoming atmosphere that makes customers want to take their time and shop. You might consider supplying refreshments and snacks. You can also use music and lighting to set the mood for a pleasurable experience. Be accessible, but never hover. All staff members should work as a team so that buyers don't sense that your service staff is competing for their attention and their sales dollars.

Point 2: Customer service is about focusing on the emotional benefits of your product.

Buying a house is not nearly as compelling for a potential customer as living a rewarding lifestyle. The Green Company focuses on the benefits that its communities offer, then maximizes the impact of those benefits by helping its customers create their dream lifestyle. By focusing your attention on the benefits that your company or your product offers, you can satisfy your customers' emotional desires and develop long-term loyalty.

Point 3: Customer service is about managing expectations.

You may be tempted to gloss over the typical glitches that can happen before a transaction is complete. However, if you set realistic expectations up front, customers are more likely to handle issues with ease. Underpromise and overdeliver. Let customers know what to expect and you'll set them up to feel calm and comforted, even when things aren't going perfectly.

Point 4: Customer service is about the customer's perception, not yours.

Make a habit of asking customers what they think. Your idea of great service may be completely different from theirs. Take time to listen and adjust the way you provide service to help them come to the right conclusions. The Green Company may be 100 percent certain that its homes are 100 percent complete at closing, but until the customer agrees, they don't close.

Point 5: Customer service is about doing the right thing.

At the Green Company, employees are encouraged to do the right thing, even if it costs the company money and time. Weekly meetings that bring employees together to discuss the customer experience help to reinforce the company culture. Everyone learns from the examples brought to the table. People hear stories from senior-level managers about how they manage customer relationships. This exposure builds confidence in less experienced employees as they learn how to handle challenges. Maximizing communication within the company puts you in a better position to do the right thing for your customers.

Point 6: Customer service is about continuous points of contact.

Keeping customers happy in the long term requires an across-the-board initiative to stay in communication every step of the way. All the outstanding efforts of your sales department can be undone by a lack of responsiveness when the customer's order moves to production. When service providers follow their customers from one department to the next, they are more likely to earn positive long-term relationships. Tracking customer interactions and having a contact person assigned for each transaction all the way through means that customers are more likely to feel connected and cared about. That translates into a lasting relationship.

Point 7: Customer service is about maintaining the relationship during and after the sale.

The Green Company created the Residential Services group to offer ongoing repair and maintenance assistance to its customers. In addition, it remains helpful when past customers call with questions and requests. You can mimic its approach by making the decision to solve your customers' problems and offer assistance whenever you can. Find ways to continue a relationship after the sale. Send cards and e-mails with information that may interest your past customers. Keep notes on them so that you can be quick to answer their questions when they call. Your care and attention will create an emotional connection that will keep customers coming back.

PROGRESS CHECKLIST

As you read the following checklist, rate yourself on a scale from one to ten. Are you applying the lessons you learned from the Green Company? What can you do starting now to bring your long-term customer care up a notch in each category?

1–2–3–4–5–6–7–8–9–10

_____ Offer low pressure and high pleasure.

_____ Focus on the benefits.

_____ Manage the customers' expectations.

_____ Consider your customers' perceptions.

_____ Do the right thing.

_____ Offer continuous points of contact.

_____ Maintain the relationship during and after the sale.

LESSONS LEARNED

The story of the Green Company presents many examples of how viewing customer service as a long-term proposition builds your reputation and sustainability, even during tough economic times. To help you identify and develop the building blocks of this case study, read through the following questions. Answer each one for yourself before reading our responses to see how much understanding you've already gained.

1.   Is it realistic to expect members of the customer service staff to honestly care about customers?

_____

_____

_____

_____

_____

2.   How can you enroll your satisfied customers to help you sell to new prospects?

_____

_____

_____

_____

_____

3.   What should you do if your company consistently misses deadlines?

_____

_____

_____

_____

_____

4. How do you stay calm when you have bad news to deliver?

_____

_____

_____

_____

_____

5. What do you need to do, emotionally and logistically, to follow up and follow through?

_____

_____

_____

_____

_____

6. How does your attitude affect your level of service?

_____

_____

_____

_____

_____

7. How can you increase your referrals?

_____

_____

_____

_____

_____

ANSWERS

1. **Is it realistic to expect members of the customer service staff to honestly care about customers?**

    It can be, as long as you have the right people in the right positions. Not everyone honestly cares about other people. The members of a Green Company's construction team, of their own accord, chose to sift through a garbage dumpster to find a wallet for a virtual stranger. Why would they do that? They got personal fulfillment from doing the right thing for a fellow human being. Personality types play a major part in whether you and your staff truly care about customers. Selecting people who get pleasure from helping others for positions that require high levels of customer contact is a useful way to ensure caring service.

2. **How can you enroll your satisfied customers to help you sell to new prospects?**

    Create opportunities to bring customers and prospects together. Host special events that offer value to both past and future clients. Offer activities that encourage interaction. Be brave and ask your customers to share their experiences with your new prospects. When customers are happy, they are more than willing to spread the good news about your company.

3. **What should you do if your company consistently misses deadlines?**

    Don't overpromise. Learn from the mistakes of the past, and provide realistic timetables. Analyze the process to see where the breakdowns are, and enroll those involved in production to work with you to develop accurate time measurements. When a deadline is missed, do a postmortem analysis to determine what happened and how you can prevent it from recurring. Then put systems in place to solve the problem.

4. **How do you stay calm when you have bad news to deliver?**

    Service providers get uncomfortable about delivering bad news because they don't want to deal with the customer's displeasure. The more uncomfortable you are, the more upsetting the situation becomes for your buyers. Keep in mind that people tend to mirror emotions. If you are firm, caring, and calm in the face of a customer's outrage, it will be much easier for that customer to calm down, too.

5. **What do you need to do, emotionally and logistically, to follow up and follow through?**

   Lois at the Green Company considers follow-up and follow-through to be the definition of customer service. Being nice is wonderful, but if you don't follow up with action and completion, customers lose their faith in you. Make sure you have the tools you need to be successful. Notice where you're tripping up. Do you need project management software to keep the process organized on your computer? Do you need a procedure for moving a customer through the buying process flawlessly? Put your tools in place and customer satisfaction will grow.

6. **How does your attitude affect your level of service?**

   The Green Company's chairman, Alan Green, is not above sweeping the floor. Having a "can do" attitude makes a huge difference in how customers respond to you. However, the truth is that there will be times when you don't feel good or you're in a bad mood. During those times, manage your mood so that it does not rub off on the customer. Like an actor in a movie, give the best performance you can. In the process of acting friendly, you'll start to feel friendly, and this can often lift your mood on the spot.

7. **How can you increase your referrals?**

   Your best referrals come from happy customers, but they won't refer you if they have forgotten about you. Once the service is over, it doesn't mean that the relationship is over. The Green Company opened up a Residential Services Department to offer ongoing service at a nominal price. Look for value-added, nonintrusive ways to stay top-of-mind with your past customers, like sending a regularly published educational e-mail or writing instructional articles about your industry for trade magazines.

WHO'S YOUR GLADYS?

When you have a flustered customer who doesn't understand how things work or who has limitations caused by health or extenuating circumstances, will you send her up the ladder on her own? Or will you climb it yourself instead, as Lois did? When you show that you care even after the sale, you stay top of mind for customer referrals.

CHAPTER 7

Preston Wynne Spa: Massaging Egos

Preston Wynne Spa, an award-winning spa located in Saratoga, California, knows that great customer service is an inside job. Its responsive approach to service is based on hiring the right people for the right jobs, then encouraging their growth with training, strong internal communication, and regular reminders of what works. During our interviews with company CEO Peggy Wynne Borgman, she shared how the strict attention that she pays to hiring, training, and communicating with her staff is parlayed into excellent service for her customers. Preston Wynne creates an extraordinary experience for patrons that has spa owners across the country requesting training from the consulting arm of Peggy's business. You'll discover how Preston Wynne Spa massages not only the bodies but the minds of its patrons by learning how to identify and respond to customers' social styles.

When they walk through the doors of Preston Wynne Spa, customers feel an instant sense of tranquility. The soothing earthy décor, with soft ambient lighting, sets the mood for the warm greeting each guest receives within five seconds.

Since opening the spa in 1984, owner and CEO Peggy Wynne Borgman has known that lasting impressions are made from the moment customers first arrive. She has developed stringent standards for greeting guests. "It has to be friendly, and it has to be fast, so that the client doesn't feel neglected," she explained. "There has to be eye contact and a smile."

Visiting a spa for the first time can be a bit intimidating. It takes a high-quality environment and warm, friendly staff to get clients to let their guard down and relax. At Preston Wynne, returning customers are greeted by name and welcomed back. When new patrons arrive or people come in with gift certificates, the staff members at the front desk never assume that they know what to do. The concierge says, "Welcome to Preston Wynne," and guides them through the next stage of their experience.

"We have clients that have been coming to us for 25 years," Peggy shared. "We have some clients that are the children of the children of an original client." While the demographic of spa clientele includes both males and females of a diverse age range, it's dominated by women in their mid-thirties and forties. About 80 percent are high-powered women who have the means to pay for an extravagant spa experience but are time-impoverished. The spa is a refuge from their fast-paced existence.

Clients have significant expectations, so every interaction is meticulously considered. Peggy instructs her staff of 80 employees to keep conversation natural, not scripted. At one time, scripted conversations were a service industry standard, but an overreliance on scripting has made customers intolerant of it.

Peggy experienced scripted service firsthand while having lunch at a five-star restaurant in Laguna Beach. A bird was hopping around, and it landed on her outdoor table and left a little pile. She flagged down her waiter and asked, "Would you mind cleaning it up for us?" Using a scripted response, he said, "My pleasure!" Peggy touched his arm and said, "This could not possibly bring you pleasure."

"It was so scripted," she noted. "It would have been so much better to have a real response rather than a parroted response. It was almost worse than nothing."

Peggy recalled hearing the CEO of Auberge Resorts explain that at the five-star level, you cannot script; you have to train and retrain good people. Auberge Resorts, a collection of hotels and resorts located around the world, has earned several awards for its hospitality over the years, including landing a spot on *Condé Nast Traveler*'s "Gold List of World's Best Places to Stay" in 2008. With an average daily room rate of $1,000 per night, it attracts the most discerning customers. "At a certain level, scripting is good enough," Peggy shared. "It is an upgrade. But at the higher levels, it's not good enough."

HIRE THE RIGHT PEOPLE TO CREATE THE BEST CUSTOMER EXPERIENCE

Peggy understands that excellent customer service starts with careful employee selection. She believes in a "slow to hire, quick to fire" philosophy. "There's only so much you can tell at an interview," she explained. "Some people are extremely good at the interview, but that doesn't mean they will give good service to your clients or get along well with their coworkers."

To increase the odds of making the right employee decisions, potential new hires at the spa are interviewed by both management and staff. Management seriously considers the staff's opinions before making a selection. This empowers coworkers to assume ownership of new hires, so they're more likely to form good relationships from the start.

It was a three-and-a-half-month process for Peggy to hire her director of spa operations, Nandita Mahadevan, in 2006. Nandita is in her late twenties, and in addition to her stellar education in hospitality management and her practical work experience, she has one thing that Peggy considers essential—high self-esteem.

Peggy seeks out happy, humble people with strong self-esteem because she feels that it's a key quality for providing world-class customer care. It requires an incredible amount of emotional resilience to put your ego aside and understand that when a client gets upset or a coworker is brisk with you, it's not personal. "People with low self-esteem or self-confidence burn out at customer service quickly," Peggy shared. "They might be able to give a good approximation of it or a 'burlesque' of it—like a customer service show—but it isn't heartfelt."

When it comes to the ability to provide customer care, Peggy finds that people fall into one of three categories. "Some people just have it, some people can develop it, and others never get it. Those that don't have it need to find another line of work," Peggy suggested. "I was at a five-star hotel last night being waited on by someone who didn't have the right stuff. It wasn't like someone having a bad day; it was someone having a bad career choice." Customer service is not the right line of work for everyone.

Some people need time to develop their potential. Lack of maturity or life experiences may cause them to take negative customer interactions personally. For example, Peggy hired a 20-year-old woman who was inexperienced but had potential. Over the course of a year, she blossomed. She started out like a deer in the headlights. She was shy, and her greetings on the phone were delivered in a monotone voice. She was fearful as she tried to adapt to her new job responsibilities. She had a challenging job, requiring a great deal of memorization and computer skills.

But once her training took hold and she started to connect with the spa's customer service mentality, it was like a lightbulb went on. She recognized the meaning behind her actions, and she began to relate to the client experience. "It's like building a giant building," Peggy said, using a modern twist on a classic story. "You can't see the whole thing that you're constructing. Maybe you're just building one particular part of it. Then one day you go up in a plane and say, 'Wow! It's a cathedral!'"

Peggy enjoyed watching the young woman's confidence grow. It showed in her phone interactions and in the way she began greeting guests. "She smiled more. She made more eye contact. There was so much more spirit. It was exciting to see. It's been like watching someone growing up into a new way of relating to the world," Peggy said with awe.

Many of the young women Peggy interviews don't have the inherent confidence that their position requires. "When you put them in front of the high-octane, type A, 'masters of the universe' type of folks that are a large part of our clientele, it throws them," she said. "You take someone who's not sure of herself, or whose self-esteem is a bit wobbly, and you put her with someone who is nothing but confident and used to getting his way. Then that employee is going to feel put upon or disrespected."

Watching her youngest concierge staff members get comfortable with the highly personal interactions inherent to the spa industry is rewarding to Peggy. Developing the confidence and poise to hold their own in a one-on-one interaction takes practice. "Coming from a lifestyle that relies on social media like texting and online communication, there's a separation that makes it comfortable to say things you'd never say face to face," Peggy observed. "They aren't prepared for how different it is to interact with people in person and deal with customer expectations effectively." There are many moments in customer service when you don't feel appreciated, heard, or respected. Some people are better prepared to deal with that than others.

At Preston Wynne, the hiring process starts by listening to the way potential candidates answer calculated, revealing questions. They're asked, "Can you tell me about the worst customer you ever dealt with?" The meaning they attribute to their experience is vital information for Peggy. One potential hire might say, "I learned from that experience that to be successful with that type of customer, I have to do such and such," while another might say, "I felt really disrespected, and that's why I quit that job."

Peggy's not so interested in finding out what happened; she wants to know what meaning the candidate drew from it. It's a critical part of her interview process, as the candidate's answer helps her decide who will respond well to challenging customer service situations. "People will tell you an amazing amount about themselves in those stories if you take them back to that emotional place. I don't want to know intellectually what they thought about the experience. I want to know how it made them feel," Peggy shared. "It's the emotions that they will be acting from on the job. I need to disqualify anybody who isn't going to be able to handle it."

Peggy has had several employees over the years who were fantastic with external customers but dreadful with coworkers. A classic coworker issue in the spa industry occurs between the staff members giving the treatments and the front desk concierges. The concierge staff serves two masters: the clients and the people who provide the treatments. Sometimes those two groups are at cross-purposes. A client might ask to come in late, and the therapists and aestheticians aren't happy to have their schedules thrown off. The front desk staff has to balance the needs of coworkers with the needs of the guests.

Gifted aestheticians develop a loyal following of customers who compliment them and seem to believe they can do no wrong. On occasion, this goes to someone's head, and he becomes intolerable to his coworkers, treating them like underlings. This type of behavior ultimately undermines the quality of customer interactions.

Since issues of this nature are common in her industry, Peggy is prepared to take immediate action when she sees the warning signs. When the right person is on the job, a quick reminder conversation with a manager is typically all it takes to get the employee back on track.

EMPLOYEES EXCEL WHEN THEY KNOW WHAT'S IMPORTANT

Training is the next step in developing a staff that is highly responsive to customers. Peggy created a full-day workshop that introduces new hires to the company culture. The first order of business is a discussion of the question, "What are the values that would enable somebody to give great customer service?" By talking through this question, new staff members reinforce and discern the spa's values. As Peggy explained it, "You can't take someone who doesn't share your core values and have it work."

Preston Wynne Spa has zeroed in on three core values: "Wow our customers 100 percent of the time, build and protect a fun and harmonious work environment, and achieve our goals, both personal and professional."

Money is not the top motivator for a job in hospitality. "It's generally about fifth on the list, and for some, it's number twenty. The main reason people work for us is because they love their coworkers," Peggy noted, a fact she learned through an annual employee survey. "It's really a labor of love in hospitality."

Employees at Preston Wynne enjoy coming to work. Given that such a significant portion of an employee's life is spent there, having a core value of protecting an enjoyable and harmonious work environment makes this company all the more appealing. The number one comment that new hires make after the first week or two is, "Everyone here is so nice!" They think it's a coincidence, an anomaly, or even a miracle, but it's definitely the result of Peggy's core values training.

"To put on the show that we do every day, it doesn't take much for people to fall off the high wire. It can be the one bad apple," Peggy pointed out. "One of the things we emphasize in the training is, 'If you're not part of the solution, you're part of the problem.' It's a cliché, but it's true. If you are sitting at a break table moaning about something you don't like, it's destructive."

How does Peggy help employees keep from slipping into negativity? She reminds them that they all come to work to have a great day and be happy while making money. Venting steam ruins their day. "You don't have that right," Peggy insisted. "You do have the right to complain, but you need to complain to the right people. You need to tell someone who can help you solve your problem." She is quick to add, "If you don't think there is anyone in the company who can help you solve your problem, then you need to leave."

It's a bit cynical, but it's true. As an employer, you aren't doing a negative employee any favors by keeping her. And she isn't doing your company any favors by sticking around. High-quality customer service calls for people who are committed to creating a positive client experience. Anyone who doesn't fit the culture is better off moving to an industry in which she can excel. Peggy is quick to protect employees from those who pollute the harmonious environment with constant complaining or other toxic behavior.

Peggy views the first 30 days of employment as a honeymoon period. The employee thinks the company is fabulous, and the company thinks its new hire is fabulous. Therefore, according to Peggy, if you have problems with someone early on, things never get better. This is a lesson that it takes her a long time to teach to new managers, especially when they put extensive time and energy into selecting and hiring someone.

"When a manager shakes her head and says, 'I don't know about so and so,' I ask, 'How long has it been?' If he says, 'Two weeks; I want to give her a little more time,' I'll say, 'Okay, but don't give her too much time. It's just that much less time for you to find the perfect person for that job.'" It's competitive to find staff. The industry's number one problem is finding enough qualified people to staff all the open positions, which is why many large spa organizations are operating their own schools.

CONTINUOUS LEARNING GROWS CUSTOMER SATISFACTION

To learn how to respond well to clients, employees need to be able to read people. At Preston Wynne, they learn to observe customers' social styles. There are several systems for categorizing customer behavior. Peggy uses one that outlines four basic styles that employees are trained to notice in themselves and their customers: the "Driver," the "Analytical," the "Expressive," and the "Amiable." Everyone tends to filter everyone else's behavior through his own social style. By looking and listening for patterns, employees can drop their negative judgment of patrons who have a style that is different from their own.

Drivers tend to be direct, action-oriented, and focused on results. Analyticals tend to be systematic, detail-oriented, and organized. Expressives are the chatty social butterflies, enthusiastic and with high energy. Amiable types are relationship-driven, easygoing, and friendly. While everyone can stretch into any one of these styles, people tend to have a propensity for some over the others.

Much of the spa staff leans toward the Amiable style, though some massage therapists have a bit of Analytical, which creates their interest in the mechanics of the body. "Some have more Expressive styles, perhaps garnering the occasional complaint from clients about chitchat in the treatment room, but logging the best retail ratios," Peggy shared in an article she wrote for spa professionals. "You will rarely find the Driver type in a massage room—at least, not for long. They're the ones planning to open their own facility."

In their training, the staff members learn how best to deal with the different styles, particularly the Driver style, which can be found in many of the spa's customers who are high-powered, affluent, and stressed. Once employees learn to reinterpret what at first seems like an undesirable behavior, they can better manage their own internal reaction and serve in a more positive way:

"She's not being mean; she's being direct because she's the Driver type."

"She isn't talking too much; she's an Expressive."

"This client doesn't want to reschedule right away because her style is Analytical and she's going to want to think about this."

The staff members learned that it's helpful to say to an Expressive, "Go ahead and schedule your next visit now; that way you'll have the time you want. You can always call back and cancel if it doesn't work out." They wouldn't expect the Analytical to guess at an appointment date. Analyticals value accuracy and will want to call back after they have checked their schedule.

When front-line staff members learn to observe body language, practice mood management, and respond appropriately to different communication styles, they are better prepared to deliver excellent customer care.

GIVING A CONSISTENT HIGH-QUALITY PERFORMANCE TAKES PRACTICE

Peggy has designed a five-hour training course with Holly Stiel, a well-respected service and hospitality expert. Their program was named "Selvice," because it marries sales and service in perfect harmony. Holly reinforces Peggy's message by comparing the start of a workday to the start of a performance. "Your uniform is your service costume, and your workplace is the stage. To give great service, it's helpful to consider yourself an actor playing a role with as much sincerity as possible," Holly advised. "Having a deep understanding of the perspective that goes into the role and choosing your reaction is the foundation of great service."

The service part of the training requires the spa staff to let go of what doesn't work. One of the most challenging habits that service providers need to break is the need to prove themselves right. "Being right is the booby prize," Holly shared. "It's where service breaks down. Suppose a customer is 15 minutes late for an appointment but still wants the full service time. If the concierge said, 'You're the one who's late,' she would be right, but what does it accomplish other than to anger and alienate her customer?"

Instead of reacting to a challenging customer with initial negative feelings, Holly and Peggy taught spa staff members to choose an approach that is more appropriate to their client service role.

Employees learn positive approaches to challenging situations by role playing. This portion of their training helps them gain both competency and confidence. It also dispels any fear they may have of the sales aspect of their position. Though sales and service go hand in hand, it takes a service-minded approach to sidestep "pushy" or "overbearing" behavior. "When you think back to the best service experiences you've ever had," Peggy explained, "they usually involved somebody anticipating your needs and being proactive." At Preston Wynne Spa, the staff members are comfortable suggesting products because they've practiced.

STRONG AND ONGOING INTERNAL COMMUNICATION CREATES GREAT SERVICE

Every day at Preston Wynne Spa starts with a quick preshift huddle. All workers gather with the manager on duty and set their play for the day. It's similar to what restaurants call "the lineup," and it is not unlike a football huddle. The staff members talk about any VIP customers that will be coming in or discuss how they should approach a previously un-happy patron who is coming back for a redo. It takes just a couple of minutes for the manager to create the preshift plan, and it puts everybody in alignment before starting the shift.

This daily event puts a positive focus on company basics. It builds greater awareness of the value of both customers and coworkers. It also provides tools for dealing with situations that may arise unexpectedly and sets a positive emotional state for the staff. The shift manager finds out if anyone is missing or coming in late. Managers also get the opportunity to receive employee comments.

This type of continuous communication is what Operations Director Nandita believes is responsible for the spa's low turnover rate. And a low turnover rate means that customers are more likely to have a positive experience with a well-trained and service-oriented staff member. Nandita supports her employees in their client care effort by keeping the lines of communication open. "I have an open-door policy," Nandita stated. "When issues come up, I encourage employees to talk to us so that we can get them resolved quickly."

One way to keep in contact is through technology. When there's a need, the staff can send Nandita an instant message through the spa's computer network from anywhere in the building. If a technician wants to pick up an extra shift, Nandita can look at the schedule book and reply in seconds. "I try my level best to get back to every employee immediately," she said.

Along with immediate availability through instant messaging technology, face-to-face management is a proactive step that Nandita takes every day. "Managing by walking around is the best way," she said. "It makes it easier for someone to come up to you with a problem, instead of having to track you down in your office to get the smallest things solved." Sometimes Nandita will get spa treatments herself, so she gets yet another opportunity to interact with the technicians.

About once a month, every employee receives a 10-minute review to go over his sales and performance. With an empathetic approach, Nandita touches base to ask if there are any areas where help is needed.

In spite of Nandita's efforts, there are some issues that are uncomfortable for staff to share face to face. To receive feedback on those items, Nandita provides Quality Building Report (QBR) forms to her staff. If a technician is unhappy with something or had a bad experience with a client or coworker and wants to bring it to management's attention, she can anonymously fill out a QBR form. The forms cover anything and everything, from tips being delayed to room cleanliness.

"As trivial as that may seem, that's what they do on a day-to-day basis," Nandita empathized. "When you spend eight hours in a room, its cleanliness is so important." Her deep understanding of what is meaningful to her staff is what makes Nandita an internal customer service superstar. She maintains a happy staff roster by reminding her employees, "The only way we can make things better for you is if you tell us." When employees communicate well with management, good feelings spread out to their external customers.

Preston Wynne Spa offers internal promotions for employees to boost performance and sales. The motto for one quarter was "come again," a program to increase client retention. The person from each department who received the most repeat requests was sent to a different spa for the entire day. In other months, employees received hefty gas cards or dinner for two at a fabulous restaurant. The employees were so engaged that they started to recommend promotion ideas. Nandita listened. She realized that promotions that her employees choose for themselves are more likely to be successful, because they give employees ownership of their actions.

Nandita listens to customers the same way she listens to her staff—by seeking out their thoughts and opinions. When new technicians are brought in, she often offers a free service to get customers' impressions of the new hire. This both empowers clients, who feel valued and heard, and exposes them to new services. This tactic also generates more business from existing patrons.

When asked where she gained the emotional maturity to handle a large staff with such finesse while she's still in her twenties, Nandita didn't hesitate to say, "I had fabulous bosses who let me make mistakes and learn from them." It's what she credits for her ability to listen deeply and respond appropriately to her staff and customer comments.

EVALUATE SERVICE FROM THE CUSTOMER'S POINT OF VIEW

To ensure that excellent customer service remains intact, Peggy uses "secret shoppers." These are clients who are treated to a free spa service or professionals who are skilled at evaluating staff. Their feedback gives her a detailed customer's view of what's really happening at Preston Wynne and provides information about the strengths and weaknesses of her staff. Her favorite secret shoppers are those who have previously had a complaint about the spa's services. She personally contacts them and invites them to enjoy a complimentary service and review their experience.

"It helps us develop a really good relationship," Peggy explained. "Another good side effect is that when you put an evaluation form in someone's hands, he sees everything that you've done right."

Preston Wynne's evaluation form is seven pages long. There are so many points to rate that when service is provided well, customers would have never even noticed most of the listed elements. If a customer was unhappy with one aspect of the spa's service, she has the opportunity to see the multitude of other things that have been done with excellence. It's an eye-opening experience. It's common for Peggy to receive a comment on the evaluation form that says, "I had no idea that so much is involved."

Peggy also takes time to put on her own guest goggles. On occasion, she spends a half-day at her own spa experiencing a body treatment, massage, or facial, followed by lunch and a makeup application. "I'm really impressed with our service," she affirmed.

Expressing gratitude to the people who make that happen is important to Peggy. She admits that as a business owner, she tends to be hard on people and hard on herself, too. After the pleasure of experiencing her spa from a customer perceptive, she finds time to talk to each person, filling out a secret shopper form for each so that she can share everything that they are doing right.

MAKE SURE CUSTOMERS LEAVE HAPPY

"Making sure the client walks out happy is the most important thing we can do," said Nandita. How do Preston Wynne employees measure happiness? They have several specific ways, including rating cards at the front desk. "The little cards are easy for customers to fill out quickly, and each week we look at those scores," Peggy explained.

Clients rate the spa service providers, the facilities, and the environment. A score of 7 or below is considered unacceptable. "We pay a lot of attention to those scores," said Peggy. "Clients are always giving us great ideas, and we also get a lot of praise for our employees. It's a pipeline of feedback from guests to employees."

Until they know that the client is happy, Preston Wynne employees haven't finished their job. The concierge staff is instructed to ask questions before customers leave the spa to gauge their satisfaction. They use an easy, low-pressure way to inquire.

They know better than to simply ask, "How was everything?" People sometimes don't feel comfortable answering that question honestly. Preston Wynne clients are asked a more useful question, like "How did you enjoy your Ocean Glow with Natalie today?" Most people won't say, "Fine," if they are really happy. Most people will say, "It was fantastic," or "She was great," or even, "I can't wait to do it again."

When customers give one-word responses like "fine" or "good," the concierge is instructed to ask, "What can we do to make your next treatment even better?" A question like that sidesteps the discomfort that is sometimes associated with sharing honest negative feedback. The customer can quickly and easily say, "The room could have been warmer" instead of feeling like he's complaining. The concierge is instructed to respond by promising to pass that information along to spa management.

With the many ways Preston Wynne uses to communicate and educate both its employees and its patrons, it's no wonder that customers leave the spa feeling happy, appreciated, and eager to come back again.

* * *

Now that you've read the case study for Preston Wynne Spa, how will you use internal communication and staff management to better meet the needs of employees and customers at your company? Read through the Practical Points, Progress Checklist, and Lessons Learned sections that follow and notice which ideas you are already putting to use in your own business and which ones you can adopt. Then set a goal to communicate more effectively with your clients and your staff, and create a few measurable ways to track your progress.

PRACTICAL POINTS

Point 1: Customer service is about making an instant impression.

From the moment your customers walk through the door or call your office, they're forming their first impression of your organization and how it will take care of their needs. Making sure that all clients are greeted warmly and promptly helps draw them in and create an initial connection. Paying attention to the details of your business space, from the decor to how neatly products are displayed, makes a powerful difference in your clients' perceptions of your organization.

Point 2: Customer service is about putting the right people on the job.

Not everyone excels at customer service. When interviewing potential hires, ask questions that reveal how the candidate feels about challenging customers. Does she display a natural desire to be of service? Invite employees who will work closely with the new employee to take part in the interviewing process. This will help nurture positive coworker relationships that will ultimately have a positive effect on customer relationships. While it's wise to take a slow and methodical approach to hiring, be quick to fire anyone who does not fit into your company's customer service culture. Most experienced managers agree that when there are problems with an employee early on, things are not likely to get better over time.

Point 3: Customer service is about interpreting clients' communication styles.

People generally fall into obvious communication and behavior categories. Learning about these different styles can make it easier to provide excellent customer service, no matter what type of client you're serving. Studying different aspects of human behavior, from personality styles to body language, is a great way to develop skills that will allow you to connect with all types of customers.

Point 4: Customer service is about contributing to a happy work environment.

At Preston Wynne Spa, everyone knows that if you aren't part of the solution, you're part of the problem. Encourage your employees to come up with their own solutions to any problems that may adversely affect your customers' experiences with your company. Go to the source of the problem to determine how it can be fixed. Create employee opinion surveys and encourage staff members to fill them out constructively and with honesty. Don't tolerate complaining in the workplace; empower employees to work to make things better. Encourage strong relationships with staff members so that you have a cohesive team that has the clients' best interests as a top priority. Your customers will thank you.

Point 5: Customer service is about consistently presenting an artistic service performance.

Encourage employees to think of going to work as going on stage to perform for an appreciative audience. To put on their best possible performance, they need training. Provide new employees with the knowledge they need for their role, and give constructive feedback as they develop their performance. Would you want to see a movie that featured an actor who didn't know his lines? Of course not! Make sure your customers are getting the outstanding performance they deserve.

Point 6: Customer service is about evaluating results.

Great customer service calls for ongoing evaluation. Putting gas in your car is not a one time event but an ongoing need to keep your vehicle running. Likewise, evaluating the quality of your company's customer service must be done on an ongoing basis to ensure continued success. When you put your guest goggles on, and view your company from the customers perspective, you gain the ability to tap into what is going well, and what needs to be improved. Asking for feedback from customers and coworkers through surveys and tactful inquiry will make significant strides in moving in the right direction.

Point 7: Customer service is about making sure all interactions end on a happy note.

Asking the right questions about a client's experience will get you an honest answer. For example, if you ask your client how "everything went," her answer is most likely to be, "Fine." No one wants to be seen as a complainer, particularly with smaller incidents, so many customers won't tell you that everything wasn't as it should have been. However, if you ask customers if there is anything you can do to make their experience better next time, you give them the chance to tell you what you can improve. If a client complains later, think of ways you can invite him to "secret shop" your business or offer a coupon for a repeat of the service that displeased him. It gives the customer the chance to see what you're doing right and shows him how interested you are in ensuring his happiness.

PROGRESS CHECKLIST

As you read the following checklist, rate yourself on a scale from one to ten. Are you applying the lessons you learned from Preston Wynne Spa? What can you put in place today to improve the customer experience in each category?

1-2-3-4-5-6-7-8-9-10

_____ Create an excellent first impression.

_____ Put the right people on the job.

_____ Respond positively to a variety of communication styles.

_____ Contribute to a happy work environment.

_____ Present a consistent artistic service performance.

_____ Evaluate results and make improvements.

_____ Make sure all customer interactions end on a happy note.

LESSONS LEARNED

The story of Preston Wynne Spa provides a plethora of practical ways to use communication tools—internally and externally focused—that produce delightful customer experiences. To make it easier for you to massage these tools into place at your business, read through the following questions. Answer each one for yourself before reading our responses to see how much understanding you've already gained.

1. Do scripted responses improve or detract from positive customer interactions?

   _____
   _____
   _____
   _____
   _____

2. How is it helpful to give both customers and employees active choices?

   _____
   _____
   _____
   _____
   _____

3. How do you grow your employees' customer service self-esteem?

   _____
   _____
   _____
   _____
   _____

4. How do customers benefit when core values are well communicated to front-line staff?

   _____
   _____
   _____
   _____
   _____

5. How can employees learn to turn their complaints into positive change?

    _____

    _____

    _____

    _____

    _____

6. How do you mentally prepare yourself and your staff to give a stellar performance on the job?

    _____

    _____

    _____

    _____

    _____

7. How do personal measurement systems help improve the customer experience?

    _____

    _____

    _____

    _____

    _____

ANSWERS

1. **Do scripted responses improve or detract from positive customer interactions?**

    Scripted responses can both help and hinder client interactions, depending on how they're used. If you have a common issue that recurs in your business, knowing the response that encourages a positive customer reaction is extremely helpful. For example, it's a good practice to thank a patron who brings a problem to your attention because you know that he is helping you make improvements to your business. That is an excellent way to use a scripted response. However, a scripted "thank you" in response to a customer complaint can sound insincere and insulting if the employee doesn't understand why she's saying it. A genuine response based on a thorough understanding of customer service principles is the best response.

2. **How is it helpful to give both customers and employees active choices?**

    People want control over their experiences. When you give them a choice, it empowers them and makes them feel vested in the outcome. For example, when you allow employees to have input into a hiring decision or a promotional activity, they are going to work hard to support that decision. That results in extra effort to build their relationship with a new coworker or taking a few extra steps to ensure a successful client promotion.

    Surveying your customers is a great way to determine their preferences. By giving them active choices about how to receive your services, products, and marketing offers, you can be sensitive to their preferences. Patrons then have a sense of ownership of their experiences with your company and feel more emotionally connected with it.

3. **How do you grow your employees' customer service self-esteem?**

    When your employees have healthy self-esteem, they won't feel defensive when they are dealing with an upset customer. They'll feel grounded and capable during turbulent times and experience joy in turning around a difficult situation with a client. You can encourage them to develop their own customer service self-esteem by doing their emotional homework. In the moment, guide them in recognizing their feelings as just that—feelings, not facts. By responding from a service mindset instead of an emotional one, they will naturally respond in a way that enhances the client connection. For example, if a hysterical customer demands something that your staff can't give her, responding with anger or indignation won't produce a positive result. When a service provider feels a negative emotion, it's his responsibility to manage those feelings so that he can stay focused on the desired outcome (a happy customer) and respond helpfully. Learning to manage feelings will help your employees develop a natural ability to defuse just about any situation. Taking part in personal growth workshops, reading self-development books, and role-playing common high-pressure client interactions with coworkers will help grow their customer service self-esteem.

4. **How do customers benefit when core values are well communicated to front-line staff?**

When well-defined core values are shared with employees and reinforced on a regular basis, customer service improves. Employees know what is expected of them and are accountable to those expectations. The company's values act as a compass to direct employee actions in challenging situations. And customers get consistent service regardless of which employee serves them because everyone adheres to the same set of values.

5. **How can employees learn to turn their complaints into positive change?**

Develop a solution-focused mindset. Some managers use a helpful tool for redirecting employee complaints by saying, "Don't bring me problems, bring me solutions." While this may cause employees to roll their eyes, they typically come back with a few ideas for solving the problems they have encountered. What if you used that method for yourself? It would mean encouraging your staff members to take active responsibility for making things better, while offering them more control over their work environment.

If an employee comes to you with a complaint about a coworker, encourage him to speak directly to that person to resolve the issue. For example, the massage therapist who had a problem with room cleanliness could courteously request better service from the coworker who had the responsibility for room hygiene. Only when the employee has exhausted all options would he approach management to solve the problem for him.

6. **How do you mentally prepare yourself and your staff to give a stellar performance on the job?**

   Delivering consistent and excellent customer service is an art form that is not unlike acting. You must display an abundance of positive emotions to deliver stellar service. "Acting" doesn't mean being fake; it only means staying focused on the most positive aspects of your performance. A solid performance can happen only when every cast member knows her role and all of her lines. Be the director and conduct role-playing exercises so that everyone is well rehearsed. Encourage social activities within your company to develop good rapport among the players, which improves group performance. Like an ensemble cast, everyone needs to give it all he's got if your company is to receive a standing ovation of appreciation from your customer audience.

7. **How do personal measurement systems help improve the customer experience?**

   It's common knowledge that in business, "you get what you measure." In customer service situations, that translates into measuring the clients' wants and perceptions, and having a system in place to respond to those measurements. Preston Wynne Spa does this with new customer information cards, surveys, secret shopper forms, and personal interactions. Learning what customers really feel and want, then delivering an experience that meets their expectations is the best way to create loyalty. Customer satisfaction tools also provide information that can be used to reinforce positive behavior in service providers and weed out any employees who aren't able to deliver.

WHO'S YOUR GLADYS?

She may be someone with a social style that's different from your own. Are you massaging your own ego by telling yourself that her personality is flawed? Or are you massaging your customers' egos by valuing each customer's unique way of interacting with the world? Do you have processes and systems in place so that your staff is trained to respond positively to a variety of personality types?

CHAPTER 8

ClearVision Optical: SurveyMonkey Around

ClearVision Optical (CVO), a distributor of optical products including prescription eyeglass frames and fashion sunglasses, has enjoyed steady and profitable growth since the company was founded in 1949. It has received top industry rankings in the Jobson ViewPoint Frames Performance Perceptions Report, a primary source of market data for the optical community, including "best overall service," "best customer service," and "reliability in shipping and handling of orders." Its products are marketed to adults, teenagers, and children around the world. Its customers, ranging from large national chains to local single-office eyecare professionals, are as vastly different as its markets. What impressed us the most about ClearVision was its consistent focus on two-way communication. Its executives solicit opinions in several forms from all of their constituents— consumers, customers, employees, sales agents, and vendors—and they back up what they find out with action. In this chapter, you'll discover that ClearVision management doesn't believe that a Gladys should keep her negative opinions to herself. They seek out the complainers using several feedback methods, including online survey tools like SurveyMonkey.

In the mid-2000s, ClearVision Optical's management team launched a growth plan to become one of the top five companies in its industry. "There were four giant competitors," President David Friedfeld explained. "One had a long history of product quality. One was known for its designer brands. The third was also a retailer, so it had its own distribution. And the fourth was owned by a managed-care company. We decided that ClearVision could be positioned as providing superior customer service. Our philosophy about customers is that if we give them more service than they require, they'll keep us in business."

This consistent effort to provide superior customer service ranked ClearVision in the top five in the United States in 2008 in three customer service categories of the ViewPoint survey, a national study conducted annually by Jobson Optical Research in New York. This online survey of optical retailers provides rankings of brand and company perception for optical brands, manufacturers, and distributors.

ClearVision has focused on regular two-way communication—ongoing dialogue between the company and its internal and external customers—to achieve spectacular results in customer service.

SURVEYING CUSTOMERS YIELDS VALUABLE INFORMATION FOR ACTION

David Friedfeld reads through about a thousand customer surveys every 60 days. The questionnaires are sent to 10,000 customers and are included in the company's quarterly newsletter. There are usually five multiple-choice questions and one open-ended query. Questions cover everything from a retailer's purchase of a specific style to comments about how ClearVision packages eyewear marketing materials.

"We've even had a question that compared and contrasted Clear Vision with our competitors," David noted. "We'll ask open-ended questions like, 'Is there any other service you would like that we don't offer?' We've had customers tell us that our freight and delivery system could be improved, or that they'd prefer their order confirmation through e-mail. They've also asked us to make our web site more interactive. We've listened and made changes based on those suggestions."

ClearVision uses an online survey publishing tool at Survey Monkey.com. The site allows CVO managers to "slice and dice" the information by region, type of customer, CVO sales manager or representative, and other relevant categories. This makes the information even more valuable to the company's customer service efforts.

It's the questions that encourage customers to be descriptive that fascinate David. "The answers to the subjective questions are phenomenal," he said. "When a customer has a negative opinion, it may conflict with 99 percent of what we believe. But we listen even more carefully to them." He described a response from one customer who said, "Your statement is hard to read." After talking to the customer personally, David directed his manager to review the company's statement, and it was simplified to make it easier for all customers to decipher.

David sees everything through the eyes of the customer. "My philosophy is based on the Trout and Ries book *Bottom-Up Marketing*. Trout and Ries stated that many companies are top-down, ivory tower–driven. Top-down businesses tell the customers what they need. What the authors did in this book was turn that pyramid upside down and put the customer at the top so that the customers' needs drive decisions."

The book extols the virtues of paying significant attention to the needs and wants of the customer, then creating strategies based on a thorough understanding of that information. It also recommends developing tactics and implementing them throughout the organization, rather than simply within the sales or marketing department.

USE CUSTOMER OPINIONS TO YOUR BEST ADVANTAGE

ClearVision Chief Operating Officer Steve Lachenmeyer shares David's philosophy. "Customer input is vital to our success," he said. "Other companies say, 'Customer feedback is important,' but they don't act on it. We solicit input from customers, employees, and sales consultants quarterly and monthly. But if they never see action, we lose credibility, so we are constantly executing against this feedback."

Steve described most of the requests or complaints that come from customers through the CVO surveys as fitting into one of three categories. "If they ask for something we already do, we need to communicate with them about it. An example might be a retailer who says, 'It would be great if we could get marketing material to support the BCBG line of eyewear.' We need to close that loop and let the customer know that we already offer it.

"If it's a new request or suggestion, we review it and implement it when we can. If someone is requesting something that we have considered and can't do, it can be pretty delicate. We explain it from our perspective. We acknowledge the request and explain why it's not feasible. Most customers are fine if they feel they've been treated fairly. It's an overused cliché that the customer is always right. We believe that the customer should always walk away feeling that he's been treated fairly."

When a customer provides negative feedback on a survey, David contacts her personally to talk through the issue and see what needs to be done to resolve the problem or improve the service. He spends a lot of time on these calls, but the information he receives is invaluable to the company's customer service efforts.

David also reviews the positive responses, in case a suggested change comes through. "Positive comments give great information, too," he noted. "One customer said we had a good co-op program, but he was never sure what his total was. I called him and found out that in order to find out the total sales on which his co-op allotment is based, he had to go through his invoices and add it all up. We could add total sales on the statements very easily, so we did it. The customer was ecstatic."

PERSONAL CONTACT RAISES CUSTOMER SERVICE EFFECTIVENESS

ClearVision management encourages personal contact with customers. "Every time we ship an order to a new customer, we follow up with a phone call," said Nancy Bernard, director of sales. "We ask him, 'How are we doing? Was it what you expected? Is there anything we can do better?' It gives us great information. Each time we touch a customer, we learn. It helps us better care for all of them."

Nancy believes that ClearVision's commitment to personal interaction is another reason that two-way communication with its customers is so convenient and commonplace throughout the company. "Each time a customer calls us, she gets to speak to a customer care specialist. Someone answers the phone, and the customer gets to talk to a 'real live person.' Customers love it. The conversation becomes interactive. Sometimes they're just placing an order and they ask questions. They may be confused, and having a personal conversation allows the specialist to interact with the customer. If something is bothering a customer, we address it directly with that customer to implement an immediate solution. It gets logged, and we look at those logs to correct processes and further train our employees.

"This ongoing tracked communication allows ClearVision to learn about customer needs and react proactively," she explained. "There's a service we put into place last year that is unique. It's called RX Express. We created a team of trained specialists who phone the account at a specific time and date to facilitate the next order. Our customers are busy, so we offer to call them at a time that's most convenient to them to take their orders. The reactions have been very positive."

SHOW CUSTOMERS THAT THEIR FEEDBACK MATTERS

One of ClearVision's best two-way communication tools is its customer newsletter, *Outlook*. The publication's content varies, although typically it is used to highlight new CVO products, which include frames from designers like Cole Haan, Izod, and BCBG Max Azria; or to promote services like CVO's retail furnishings and displays. The multipage print piece, which is available in both hard copy and electronic versions, uses full-color artwork so that it's bright and appealing. In the back of every issue is a survey that can be faxed in or filled out online. Customers are motivated to complete the survey through an offer of a delightful gift, like a pair of sunglasses, a leather wallet, or a pen.

Another tool that ClearVision frequently uses is customer focus groups and customer advisory panels. "In 1989, we created our Fisher-Price Eyewear line as a result of a focus group session," David Friedfeld said. "We surveyed opticians and consumers and asked them questions about what they needed. Many moms and dads said that children's eyewear was simply shrunken-down versions of adult eyewear, so the fit was wrong. We built a new collection of eyewear based on that focus group."

ClearVision created the "Fisher-Price Fit-Kit," a unique pediatric fitting kit to make it easy for its optical professional clients to properly size eyewear for preschool and early elementary school children. The Fisher-Price collection, licensed in 1988, accommodates children's facial features with a variety of colors, shapes, and sizes, so the glasses don't fall off the child's face.

TAKE ACTION ON THE INPUT AND IDEAS OF FRONT-LINE EMPLOYEES

Nancy Bernard finds that some of her best suggestions for improving customer care come from employees. "Our employees come up with the best ideas," she explained. "When we first started a co-op ad program (a plan that pays part of retailers' advertising expenditures if they advertise Clear-

Vision products), we told our customers that we would give them their percentage as a credit for free product. A lot of the customers told their customer care representatives that they would value a rebate check more. I went to David and asked him, 'If I put together a proposal, would you be open to it?' He said he would. I did the research, and we changed the way we compensated our retailers for advertising."

Nancy, who has been with the company since 1987, has a personal philosophy that makes it easy to provide the best possible service. "The customers are gold, and they have to be treated as such," she commented. "We have to understand their perspective."

ClearVision holds weekly executive team meetings, where both customer and employee suggestions are reviewed. "Our executive group reviews all the information that comes in through the communication, and plans are created," Steve Lachenmeyer added. "The executives are charged with implementing the plans. Later, we regroup and talk about those action items."

Steve had what he described as an "aha moment" early in the interview process, before he was hired by ClearVision Optical. "During the information-gathering process, when we were getting to know each other to see if it was a good fit, it became clear that ClearVision had an incredible focus on individuals. The managers there realize the value of people. They invest in trying to fully develop a person—whether it's an employee, a sales consultant, or a customer. They want to maximize opportunities for people. Then I joined the company and saw how we treat people with respect and dignity and try to make their lives better. That's really why we're good at customer service."

EMPLOYEES RESPOND TO ONGOING COMMUNICATION AND TRAINING

Nancy Bernard knows that ClearVision's employees can't serve the customer unless they have a complete understanding of the company's goals, along with proper training on how to perform their jobs. "Our communication is loud and clear, inside and out," she shared. "Everyone knows our customer care philosophy. All our employees understand that our goal is to make sure our customers are satisfied beyond their expectations."

All ClearVision employees are trained in the company's Customer

Care Performance Strategy, simply referred to as the "Four Cs." This clearly stated and widely distributed document provides a structure that, once known, can be the basis for both daily decisions and long-range planning.

"The four individual links are The Consumer, The Customer, The Caretaker, and The Community," the strategy reads. "The Four C's are linked by ClearVision's acknowledgement and in-depth understanding of customer needs and the network the company has created to respond to it. The Four C's are built on a foundation of principles and values that connect everyone involved."

The descriptive information that is distributed to employees, customers, and the media describes the Consumer as the person who buys the products that ClearVision distributes. The Customer refers to people at the independent optical retailer, both its staff and the professionals. The Caretakers are the ClearVision employees. And the Community represents the charitable and community causes that employees and leaders believe in and support. The Four Cs cover all those who must be properly cared for to ensure the company's success.

Mary Crisafulli, CVO's chief talent officer, manages ClearVision University, the company's in-house education program, and the company's internal communication efforts. To make sure that all employees understand the ClearVision culture and business goals, "We reinforce it in explicit ways. We hold a variety of employee events, including an all-employee town hall meeting every six weeks. That's when we talk about our successes and our performance. We also identify individual employees who have achieved landmarks. The key is delivering a very clear message about business goals and company culture. We even print the mission statement on each employee's security badge."

All ClearVision employees take training at ClearVision University. "Our customer care specialists get training on our products, programs, and policies, as well as internal and external customer service. Sometimes we use inside trainers and sometimes we bring in outside experts," Nancy explained.

The talent management team aims to provide a hundred hours of training annually to each employee. Topics include general customer service and sales training, as well as training on the more technical aspects of serving the customer. "We teach them how to provide value-added service. They learn what services and business support they can offer the customer," Mary noted.

High-potential employees, those employees who have shown an ability to excel beyond their peers, go through ClearVision University's "Management 101" program, receiving weekly training for three months. "We work around their job schedules and train them in customer service, production, and software," Mary explained. All ClearVision employees are offered courses in more general life skills as well, such as English as a Second Language (ESL), defensive driving, CPR, and even yoga.

TWO-WAY COMMUNICATION FACILITATES POSITIVE CHANGE

ClearVision also espouses two-way communication internally as a way to attract and retain the best employees. "We survey employees at specific intervals," Nancy explained. "While Customer Care works with our accounts, our employees and vendors are viewed as *internal customers.*"

ClearVision uses surveys and personal contact with management to get much-needed feedback from its staff members. "We get employee input on our processes and on aspects of our workspace, such as lighting, their surroundings, and our amenities," commented David Friedfeld. "Last year, we mapped all the processes of all of our employees with an outside consultant so that we could get all the information in one central area. This allowed us to see where inefficiencies are present."

David also met personally with each employee to ask him what he was doing in his position that someone in another position should do, where he saw waste and inefficiency, and what he expected from Clear Vision management. "We had four to six people in a group, without a manager, so they felt they could speak freely. We found out that people want to be treated fairly. They believe that rewards should be based on performance. The meetings confirmed their engagement with the company goals. They want leadership, including oversight, mentorship, and time, from their boss, so we added more managers. Why? Because management adds value, and that means that good employees will stay with us.

"Most importantly, employees want security and no layoffs. A few years back, we forecast that we would not make the profit that we wanted to. It came up that we should either lay off some employees, cut back on our annual charitable contributions, or stop contributing to employee profit sharing. We decided not to cut any of those items, and we agreed to lose money that year, funding these things ourselves from prior years' successes."

This valuable information about employees' wants and needs has helped Mary Crisafulli in talent management as she works with management to steer the company's growth. "As we grow, the requirements of the jobs change, particularly in the scope of work and the expectations of how departments work together," she noted. "Before, an employee did steps one through four; now she may do only one through three. Employees have to know how to gracefully hand off the parts they no longer do. Change management is a combination of continuous communication and staying connected to the workforce. We need to know where the pain points are going to arise.

"Working largely with management teams, I help them sort it out. We figure out where the gaps are and how to get the right people in the room to make change happen. We help them understand the process and how their piece of the process affects others down the line; it's process orientation and process thinking. It's so hard, because when you're doing it right, it means being willing to make a midcourse correction. We have to stay connected and not become married to the plan. We have to be willing to do it more than one way."

TLC FOR EMPLOYEES DELIVERS LOYALTY

ClearVision Optical's management team shows extensive appreciation of the company's employees for their efforts to serve their customers. If a customer compliments an employee, this is personally acknowledged by David Friedfeld. "David's involvement puts the meat behind the words," noted Mary Crisafulli. The positive message is also posted on the bulletin board in the company's "Relaxation Station," a social common area that serves as the company's "water cooler." It's a place where staff members get coffee and are often treated to company-purchased bagels and other snacks.

In addition, employees are recognized every season with a small gift. "In the fall, we had a flowerpot with a pumpkin bread mix to cook in it. We have a fall festival where we have a costume contest and guess the weight of a pumpkin. Prizes include additional time off from work. Every Thanksgiving, we hold a luncheon, and everyone gets a $40 bonus in her paycheck to help her pay for a turkey."

Throughout the year, ClearVision offers employees theater outings, trips to local attractions, holiday parties, a bagel breakfast once a month for employee birthdays, ice cream socials, and going-away parties for employees who leave the company.

This obvious gratitude for the efforts of its staff members pays off in employee loyalty and a clear understanding of the company's business goals and culture. The ongoing two-way communication also ensures that everyone is on the same page philosophically about what it takes to provide the best possible customer service.

* * *

Now that you've read the case study for ClearVision Optical, how will you create a two-way communication loop that meets the needs of both customers and coworkers at your company? Read through the Practical Points, Progress Checklist, and Lessons Learned sections that follow and notice which ideas you are already putting to use in your own business and which ones you can adopt. Set a goal of listening and responding to your customers and coworkers, then create a few measurable ways to track your progress.

PRACTICAL POINTS

Point 1: Strong customer service can differentiate you from your competitors and provide a competitive advantage.

ClearVision Optical's management team saw an opportunity to gain a competitive advantage by focusing on providing the best customer service in its industry. The use of two-way communication has allowed the company to move to the top of several of its industry's "best customer service" lists. As a result, ClearVision has increased customer retention, gained new clients, and grown steadily.

Point 2: Use customer surveys to gain valuable information about what your customers really want.

ClearVision uses customer surveys to find out what's important to its customers so that it can respond accordingly. Customers have unique wants and needs, and you can serve them best when you know what those wants and needs are. Customer feedback can also guide your marketing and product decisions, so that your business more closely matches the market's needs. ClearVision developed its successful Fisher-Price brand of eyewear for young children after discovering a need for the product through customer research.

Point 3: Respond to a customer's negative opinions with personal contact.

A customer complaint can give you crucial information that will allow you to improve your process or your product. It is always best to respond to negative feedback with a personal phone call or visit. E-mail and other written responses make it difficult, if not impossible, to read subtleties like tone or facial expression. Correspondence that gets misinterpreted can cause major communication breakdowns. Two-way, live conversation allows you to ask questions immediately and perhaps get more detailed information about your customer's suggestion or complaint.

Point 4: Be fair with customers, even when they make an unreasonable request.

Steve Lachenmeyer, ClearVision COO, said it best when he told us that "the customer is always right" is an adage that is past its prime. Even when a customer wants something that you can't give him, if you explain the reasons behind your inability to grant his wish and offer an alternative, you can typically get the relationship back on course. Feeling that they've been treated fairly is more important to most people than simply being right.

Point 5: Use a variety of feedback tools to gain the best and widest breadth of useful information.

ClearVision uses meetings, telephone calls, e-mails, customer visits, customer advisory panels, focus groups, and surveys to solicit opinions from its internal and external customers. Different types of communication may yield different results. Sometimes a quick multiple-choice survey is the best tool. In some cases, a focus group will yield more valuable qualitative information. Research the benefits of each and match the tool with your specific information needs. Using a combination of tools will give you the widest and most useful information so that you can craft your customer service effort to give maximum results. Put follow-through procedures in place to ensure that the feedback loop is closed.

Point 6: A written customer service philosophy is a requirement for superior service.

A consistent customer service effort is the best way to ensure the highest quality of service, the kind that keeps customers coming back to your company over and over again. Spend some time writing up your company's customer service philosophy. Then communicate it to your employees repeatedly. Involve your staff members so that they feel ownership in the processes to make it work. Then provide ongoing communication at staff meetings, in the company newsletter, at meetings, and any other way that fits your company's style and culture.

Point 7: Employee training and communication lift customer service quality.

Employees thrive when they know what is expected of them. Once you've spelled out your customer service philosophy, communicate it, communicate it, communicate it (over and over) to your staff. Model it with your own actions, so that employees can make any decision that arises with a clear understanding of the company's priorities. Make sure that your employees know how to do their jobs and that they've been trained in customer service. Solicit their input during meetings and with surveys. Your employees may be spending more time with your customers than you are.

PROGRESS CHECKLIST

As you read the following checklist, rate yourself on a scale from one to ten. Are you applying the lessons you learned from ClearVision Optical? What can you put in place today to get more information and ideas from your consumers, customers, and coworkers?

1–2–3–4–5–6–7–8–9–10

_____ Gain a competitive advantage by giving strong customer service.

_____ Use surveys to gain valuable information about what customers want.

_____ Respond to a customer's complaints through personal contact.

_____ Be fair, even when you think the customer is wrong.

_____ Use a wide variety of feedback tools.
_____ Communicate your customer service philosophy with
employees regularly.
_____ Give and receive ongoing training.

LESSONS LEARNED

The story of ClearVision Optical provides several practical ways to use customer feedback to produce delightful customer experiences. To help you learn how to solicit information and use it to the advantage of your customer service effort, read through the following questions. Answer each one for yourself before reading our responses to see how much understanding you've already gained.

1. Why do I need to seek out customers' opinions when I believe that I already know what my customers need?

    _____

    _____

    _____

    _____

    _____

2. Why is top management involvement in regular team meetings so critical to a company's success?

    _____

    _____

    _____

    _____

    _____

3. What should I do when a customer gives me negative feedback?

    _____

    _____

    _____

    _____

    _____

4. Why is it important to log feedback and retain feedback information for future review?

_____

_____

_____

_____

_____

5. Why is personal interaction so critical to two-way communication efforts?

_____

_____

_____

_____

_____

6. How can I communicate my company's customer service philosophy to employees and/or coworkers?

_____

_____

_____

_____

_____

7. Why should I express ongoing gratitude to my employees and/or coworkers?

_____

_____

_____

_____

_____

ANSWERS

1. **Why do I need to seek out customers' opinions when I believe that I already know what my customers need?**

    Don't always assume that you know what your customers need when it's so easy to simply ask. Two-way communication can provide opportunities to find out how your company is perceived and gain suggestions for improving your product. Customers are often flattered to be asked for their thoughts, and seeing their suggested improvements implemented creates goodwill.

2. **Why is top management involvement in regular team meetings so critical to a company's success?**

    ClearVision Optical's management team reviews customer and employee feedback during its regularly scheduled meetings. When an idea is to be implemented, one of the managers takes on the responsibility of seeing it through. Regular meetings allow managers to follow up on assigned tasks and make sure that improvement projects don't get stalled or forgotten.

3. **What should I do when a customer gives me negative feedback?**

    View customer complaints as opportunities to improve your processes, your service, or your product. A customer who complains or tells you what's really on her mind, even if it's an idea that you can't implement, is giving you valuable advice on what you could be doing better. Respond to negative feedback with a personal phone call, rather than written correspondence, so that you don't lose the nuances of voice tone and you'll have the opportunity to ask questions.

4. **Why is it important to log feedback and retain feedback information for future review?**

    Tracking feedback, both negative and positive, can help you monitor trends of improvement in your customer service effort and your processes. When negative customer comments are logged and reviewed by company management, problems can be addressed immediately and the customer relationship salvaged or even enhanced.

5. **Why is personal interaction so critical to two-way communication efforts?**

   While surveys and focus groups can yield both quantitative and qualitative information, personal interaction offers additional benefits. It's immediate, and you can instantly clarify any responses that are unclear or easily misinterpreted. You can also offer an explanation if the customer is having a problem with something that you can't remedy right away.

6. **How can I communicate my company's customer service philosophy to employees and/or coworkers?**

   Employees who know the company's customer service philosophy are better equipped to carry it out through their actions. All staff members should receive initial training on company goals and philosophies. You can then reinforce the message at staff meetings, in written correspondence, and in e-mails. Use other creative ways to communicate it that are unique to your business. ClearVision prints its mission statement on employee security badges, which are carried by all CVO staff.

7. **Why should I express ongoing gratitude to my employees and/or coworkers?**

   Talented staff members have greater opportunities to work elsewhere, as good people are always in demand. Employees who feel valued will be happier employees, which will reduce your staff turnover. You'll find that the good feelings that are generated extend to the customers. Staff retention also communicates excellence, as a customer care provider who has been with the company for a significant amount of time is typically more knowledgeable. Customers also appreciate working with someone they know.

WHO'S YOUR GLADYS?

ClearVision Optical seeks out complaints using online surveys. When a customer noted that he thought his statement was difficult to read, ClearVision managers changed the form. Do you see your complaining customers as a gift? They can give you valuable feedback so that you can make improvements that benefit all your customers.

CHAPTER 9

Sky Lakes Medical Center: Take, Don't Tell

Sky Lakes Medical Center serves nearly 120,000 people in a 10,000-square-mile area in southern Oregon and northern California. Located in Klamath Falls, Oregon, this 176-bed nationally accredited hospital has earned an exemplary reputation for medical excellence, superior skills, and advanced technology. Sky Lakes has made great strides in customer service improvement, creating a strong culture of shared values and best practices with its employees. This relatively new way of doing business puts the care of its customers—patients and their families—at the forefront of everything the hospital does. To assist it in the effort, Sky Lakes hired Custom Learning Systems (CLS), a company that provided it with the transformational tools it needed to create a sustainable change in its corporate culture. What really stood out during our interviews with Tom Hottman, Sky Lakes public information officer, and Brian Lee, CEO of CLS, was their team spirit, across-the-board accountability, and constant pursuit of patient satisfaction. "Take, don't tell" are three little words that have had a big impact at Sky Lakes. In this chapter, you will see how this simple directive creates extraordinary customer experiences.

A friendly greeting is a trademark of good customer service, but at Sky Lakes Medical Center, the "six-foot rule" has taken greetings to a whole new level. When hospital staff members pass within six feet of anyone, they are expected to make eye contact and give a warm greeting. They say, "Good morning" or, "How's your day?" If a patient is alone, they ask, "Can I help you find somebody or someplace?" The rule also applies to fellow employees. Walking past a coworker with your head down is not okay at Sky Lakes.

"It sounds like it shouldn't be that big a deal," Jason Card, a front-line employee from the Vascular Imaging Department, explained, "But I can tell you, from our standpoint, it has made a huge difference in morale. Any time you try to make a culture change, there are going to be those who just balk at it. At Sky Lakes, either you get on board, because everyone else is on board, or you become uncomfortable enough that you don't feel comfortable working here anymore. You can start improving or this probably isn't a good fit for you and you need to find another place to work."

The six-foot-rule is just one link in the chain of a successful culture change that took place at Sky Lakes Medical Center, beginning in 2002. "Since the rule started, we've had a turnover in the lower third of the bell curve, which marks the high, middle, and low performers in any organization," Jason said. "It has made this a lot more positive and fun place to work. It's been fun to see the change."

Front-line employees like Jason are empowered, and as a result, they are remarkably committed to this new approach at Sky Lakes. Their thoughtful attention to implementation and follow-through has contributed to the hospital's success. "By and large, I am happy to come to work," Jason reported.

The hospital goes to great lengths to create good feelings for both the staff and the patients. At Sky Lakes, the term *patient* refers to both the patient and her family. "Have you ever been a patient?" Tom Hottman asked. "Do you really hear everything that's told to you? As much as we would like to believe that the patient is the center of the decision making, maybe that's not so. Because of the disease process, the number of medications, and the baggage he's carrying, either medical or emotional, the patient can't be expected to do everything. That's why we rely heavily on the family."

"We take care of people" is the underlying message from everyone at Sky Lakes Medical Center. Valuing family members is part of the inclusivity that CEO Paul Stewart was striving to create when the hospital began working with CLS in 2005.

EVOLVE TO MEET THE CHANGING NEEDS OF YOUR CUSTOMERS

The hospital was originally founded in 1965. "Fast forward to roughly 2002, that's when the decision was made that we were outgrowing our space," Public Information Officer Tom Hottman explained. "We also needed to think about what we were going to do to prepare our community for the future of health care." Sky Lakes's management team knew that the industry was evolving, and that patients were becoming more selective, with higher expectations for all aspects of customer service.

After extensive customer polling and market research, a plan was created. In the years that followed, many changes took place; a major patient-focused culture change was designed, implemented, and embraced, and a new 100,000-square-foot building was added on. The hospital changed its name to Sky Lakes Medical Center in May 2007 with a new and thoughtful philosophy of Life—Healing—Peace to match its customers' desired perceptions of the service of health care.

The new building was designed to engender the new philosophy. The patient-focused building has two lush healing gardens and a private meditation room with special glass so that people can see out but not in. There are stone walkways, tables, a garden trellis, wooden benches, and a labyrinth to help people relax. Natural elements of wood, stone, water, plants, and pleasing colors are incorporated to create a peaceful healing environment.

The new building has three floors, although it's the same height as the preexisting four-story building, allowing for much higher ceilings. The hospital rooms in the new building are furnished with high-speed Internet connections, televisions, space for the patient's family, and windows that overlook the lake and the mountains. Windows were also placed on the corridor side, so that caregivers can look in on patients without having to go in and disturb them. In addition, patients can look out of the room to see if a nurse or doctor is on his way in. Public areas, like family waiting rooms, are also well appointed.

"The patient care floors have public access to computers and a variety of different waiting areas," Tom Hottman said. "It's one of the ways we show the patient and family that they're at the center of what we do."

CREATE A DETAILED PLAN AND GET EVERYONE ON BOARD

Its idyllic medical setting was not always reflected in the Sky Lakes culture, so the company's leadership team brought in an outside company to help it create a detailed plan to reach its goal for significant improvements in patient satisfaction.

A company's corporate culture can be loosely defined as "the way things are done" at the organization. It covers shared values, unwritten rules about how employees behave, the flow of information through the organization, and what is considered "right" and "wrong." It affects how a company interacts with its customers, employees, and vendors. It develops over years and is deeply ingrained. Changing a corporate culture isn't easy. It requires a conscious team effort by both employees and management.

"Paul Stewart wanted to see a new culture in which employees are working with one another, not for someone. They are not machines in a great big repair shop," Tom explained. "Our employees are clinically highly skilled or they wouldn't be here, but the culture was not terrific. But how do you turn the enterprise around, changing the culture so that people have more of a servant's heart? That's when serendipity stepped in."

Tom was sent to a regional conference hosted by Press Ganey, an industry leader that partners with health-care facilities to measure levels of customer satisfaction and improve the quality of health-care delivery. It was there that he met Brian Lee, the CEO of Custom Learning Systems. Brian is one of North America's leading experts in the field of world-class health care and patient satisfaction.

A few weeks after the conference, Paul Stewart called Tom into his office to discuss their culture change options. "I told him what I had in mind," Tom recalled. "The beauty of Custom Learning Systems's methodology is that we were able to customize. CLS showed us the path. It gave us the tools and gave us the instructions for how to use those tools, but it became *our* plan at our place using *our* best practices."

Sky Lakes underwent a three-year plan to change the company culture. Using comprehensive assessments and tools from CLS, it inspired both leaders and front-line staff to take ownership of the new way of doing things.

Being the only hospital in a large territory was a significant hurdle for getting employees engaged in adapting to the new customer service initiatives. The mindset that needed to change was: "Why do I have to do anything differently? Where else can our patients go?" "One of the first things we learned from Brian Lee and his team," Tom recalled, "was to ask ourselves, 'If our patients could choose, would they choose us?' Lightbulbs went off."

"Authorship equals ownership," Brian Lee explained. "People don't mind making changes, but they mind being changed. So if they can be the authors of their own destiny, that is crucial. I have a saying that for every hour of work you put in up front to get 'buy-in,' you get a dividend of eight hours saved in grief and disillusionment later on. That's what happens when people feel left out.

"It takes three years to change the culture of an organization. You have to go through cycles. The first year, people get comfortable with the new culture and make it their own. The second year, they're beginning to understand it. In the third year, they begin to say, 'This is the way we do things around here.'"

Three cornerstones of culture change were embraced at Sky Lakes: Total Management Engagement and Accountability; Enthusiastic, Empowered Front-Line Leadership; and Execution Excellence. "A nurse leader said something profound once," Brian recalled. "She told me, 'The moment I take my eyes off the new initiative, it reverts to what it's been.' That's true for everything. Working on patient satisfaction is a lot like shaving. If you don't do it every day, you look like a bum." The process requests that leaders gain buy-in from staff, engage everyone, and then step back and let the magic of empowerment, ownership, and collaboration unfold.

CONTINUOUS IMPROVEMENT IS PART OF EVERYONE'S JOB DESCRIPTION

As they made their way through the process of positive change, the managers of Sky Lakes determined which "best practices" they most needed. Expectations were set so that every employee, from leaders to front-line workers, owned the patient satisfaction scores that they influenced. Nursing owned nursing scores. Admitting owned admitting scores. Dietary owned dietary scores. This built-in accountability was crucial. "When everybody owns all the results, nobody owns anything," Brian explained.

Leaders were given the responsibility for staff engagement, ensuring that the employees of Sky Lakes were interested and were taking part in the quality improvement effort. "To become a provider of choice," Brian said, "you must first become an employer of choice. It's not an option. It's not either/or. It's both."

Almost every Sky Lakes leader served on a highly structured "Operationally Advanced Service Improvement System" (OASIS) team every year for three years. Each year, this team focused on the implementation of a different strategic best practice designed to improve the patient experience.

Sky Lakes management team members were held accountable through the first of the three cornerstones of the culture change process taught by CLS. Referred to as Total Management Engagement and Accountability, this program required leaders to report the progress of their OASIS team to their peers. This accountability step helped support the best practices that were implemented.

"Hospitals are the most complex delivery of a service in any field of endeavor. It's because of pain and because a traditional patient is handed off about 60 different times in a 3$\frac{1}{2}$-day stay," Brian shared. "It's complex. Sky Lakes has done a great job of initiating and working on its best practices and getting them in place."

Continuous training and strategy implementation led to a complete shift in thinking among Sky Lakes staff members. "The old paradigm is, 'I have my job. I will do my job, and every once in a while, I'll leave my job to improve things. Then, I'll go back to my job,'" he noted. "The new paradigm is the relentless pursuit of continuous improvement, the relentless pursuit of excellence, the relentless pursuit of doing things better. Your job is to continuously improve what you do."

To make ongoing improvements, Sky Lakes empowered its front-line employees, seeking their perspective and input when problems arise. "*State the problem. Solve the problem,*" Tom Hottman declared, suggesting a delightful way of summing up key practices in a headline. "The people who do the job know the job," he said. "If they are doing a job and they see a problem, involve them in stating the problem and finding the solution so that it won't be a problem anymore."

PEER-TO-PEER TRAINING HAS A HUGE EFFECT ON CUSTOMER SERVICE

Another cornerstone of the culture change that CLS brought to Sky Lakes is referred to as Enthusiastic, Empowered Front-Line Leadership. This required management team members to hand-pick high-performing front-line employees and recruit them to become Service Excellence Advisors (SEAs). SEAs are trained and given tools to deliver peer-to-peer workshops. An SEA must be a front-line employee, nonmanagement, with a commitment to greatness and a terrific attitude.

"Again, the idea was that the people who do the job know the job," Tom explained. "Let them train their peers, because they're going to have the front-line-driven credibility. We did 30 workshops with about 30 people each in roughly six weeks. We taught the remainder in the next two or three weeks. It was a full-out blitz. That got all the current employees up to speed." To practice what they learned, rapid-cycle performance improvement teams were formed within the hospital's business units. The expectation of middle managers was that they would turn the front-line employees loose to find opportunities and problems to solve.

"The first year, we had five rapid-cycle performance improvement meetings," Tom reported. "We thought that was good. Then employees came back and said, 'Why stop?' We trained a whole new set of front-line employees for another phase of the program. We said, 'Try doing one rapid-cycle performance improvement meeting a month.' Some said, 'One? Heck, we'll do five in a month.' Others suggested one every couple of months or so. In the meantime, we're monitoring the staff by using Press Ganey patient satisfaction survey data. I was personally devastated when we looked at the data and there wasn't much change. Then, all at once, things changed. We were up. I thought, 'Wow.' Even though it was only one point. The next time—up again. The quarter after that, we hit the ninety-first percentile in the nation for our inpatient patient satisfaction. The top 10 percent in the nation—that was pretty awesome."

ELEVATE YOUR HIGH-PERFORMING FRONT-LINE STAFF

Jason Card is a front-line employee who was selected to be an SEA. "It's always a feather in your cap to be asked," he acknowledged. "As the year progressed, it became more of an honor to me because not only do you get to work with good people and earn their respect, but after the workshops, people identify you as someone they can ask if they have questions, and they feel comfortable coming to you with issues and problems."

During the two-day train-the-trainer course that new SEAs are required to attend, the first three hours cover a subject that they will then teach their peers. The content is based on Sky Lakes's most recent patient satisfaction survey. The "priority dissatisfiers," the main areas about which patients report negative comments, are identified by the outside company that administers the patient surveys and provides the results to

Sky Lakes management. The rest of the two-day training teaches SEAs how to present the material to their peers.

"We're talking about nurses, housekeepers, electricians, accountants, and lab techs who have never spoken in front of an audience before. It's a huge stretch," Brian Lee said. "Keep in mind that speaking in front of audiences is the number one fear for 44 percent of Americans, ahead of death. And what we're doing works. It's very empowering."

CLS Implementation Specialist David Dworski trained SEAs and residents at Sky Lakes over a three-year period. He was impressed with how quickly the culture change caught on with employees. He was also struck by their unique population.

"We're a small rural community," Tom Hottman explained. "It could very well be that the person you're taking care of is your son's Little League coach or your coworker's aunt. It's very possible that you're going to know who that patient is. You wouldn't treat a friend poorly. You don't want your mom to go some place that's only average. We're going to do the best we can to make sure you get great care."

In the train-the-trainer courses, David Dworski reinforced the emotional component of providing exceptional customer service to patients. "When you become a patient in the hospital, your identity is taken away from you. You're away from your family when you need their support. You're wearing weird pajama coats. How the staff treats you makes a difference," he remarked. "Patients feel loneliness, anxiety, and pain. Staff members need to be attuned to the emotional stuff. When people are in the hospital, they are not at their best. If you don't get this, look for a different line of work. Don't be a health-care professional."

David was adamant that, "You cannot motivate people. What you can do is help people come to conclusions themselves. To do that, you pose questions, share ideas, and build consensus."

"What I got from David, besides the material, was the dire importance of knowing the topic and believing it in order to sell it," Sky Lakes SEA Jason Card added. "I was very impressed that there wasn't a single question that people asked him that he didn't answer directly or spin into a topic he knew a lot about. It also impressed me that he gave all of us his personal office number. He said, 'If you ever have a question and there isn't anybody around to answer it, call me.' He wanted you to do well, and it wasn't because he would get paid more if you did.

"We do the same thing for the people we train," Jason said, referring to the SEAs at Sky Lakes. "If any of our staff members, as part of any workshop we teach, has a question, we give them a list of SEAs to call. If you can't find someone who taught your class, there's a whole list, and if you can't find someone on the list, then ask any senior management person. There was a senior management person that concluded every workshop. There was a director in every workshop. We tell them, if you have a question, need anything, or want anything, please come and find us. That attitude of David's, and his passion for the subject, was the best thing I took out of it. I think that's had the biggest impact on our customized program."

To help develop the training curriculum, Sky Lakes sat down with the people from Custom Learning Services each of the three years during the culture change. "They tailored it to us," Jason explained. "Now we're developing the entire curriculum ourselves."

"The SEAs teach in teams of four, and just like the OASIS teams, they have cross-collaboration with these front-line leaders," Brian Lee said. "They each teach a three-hour workshop. Each SEA facilitates a monthly Daily Ongoing Implementation Tactics (DO IT) meeting. Each of them works toward breaking down the 'us versus them' disconnect because everyone is on the same side of the table. It really does affect a culture change. There's an old cliché that says that one bad apple spoils the whole bunch, but one good apple can transform a whole bunch, and it shows. That's exactly what happened at Sky Lakes."

Jason has been inspired by the positive effect of his team's DO IT meetings. "We're paying a lot more attention to detail with the ongoing daily stuff," he shared, "trying to get everybody on the same team and eliminating turf wars. Even though answering the call light is probably the certified nursing assistant's job, if you're walking by and the person looks like he needs help, we stop in and say, 'Hey, is there anything I can do for you while your nurse is busy?' Sometimes you'll walk by and see that someone is trying to get up by herself or has dropped her glasses and can't reach them. That's why she pressed the call button. If you're not qualified to help her, you can at least go in and say, 'I'm sorry your nurse is busy, but he'll be in here as soon as he possibly can. Can I make you more comfortable until he can get in here to help you?' We encourage that at all levels, and it has made a huge difference."

As a front-line staff member, Jason noticed that it took some time to hard-wire the process, but he hears a lot less of the formerly common comment, "That's not my job." The attitude that prevails on the front line is, "We are here for the patients first and foremost."

EVERY EMPLOYEE CONTRIBUTES TO THE CUSTOMER EXPERIENCE

At Sky Lakes, even if employees do not give direct patient care, they are still recognized for the difference they make to the patient's experience. "We've put in a lot of time in the workshops reaffirming that the work they do in the organization makes it possible for the people giving direct patient care to do their jobs," Jason explained.

"For example, if you have a nurse who seems to think that she is the most important link in the chain and treats other coworkers accordingly, you need to show her the bigger picture. When you come right down to it, there is no way she could do her job if the linen wasn't stocked, and the people from the pharmacy didn't come up and give her the tools that she needed to do it, and diagnostic imagining wasn't coming up and providing the look inside that the doctor needs to diagnose things. So there isn't a link in the chain that doesn't have some effect on the patient. We have been reaffirming that to make sure the support staff feels appreciated. We remind anyone who loses sight of that. They really are just as important as anybody else."

Five people out of each SEA group volunteer to form what's referred to as the "Fab Five." These five individuals assist the SEA super coaches and have a few more responsibilities. They are required to put in a little more time and effort, especially up front, to help out the group. They tend to be dynamic speakers who are comfortable being in front of people. They can fill in for another SEA's workshop.

"Someone can call you in the morning and say, 'Hey, one of our presenters is sick; can you come up at 2:30 and fill in?'" Jason said. "So rather than just learn your part, you have to learn the whole thing."

Jason loves to learn. "I think that when you stop learning, that's when you die. I work mostly with elderly folks. The ones I see that are around 60 and in really bad shape, a lot of them are fairly sedentary people. Most of the 85- and 90-year-olds that are doing well are still active, reading, and working to a certain degree."

Sky Lakes's training curriculum isn't focused solely on taking care of patients. Some workshops focus on how staff members can take care of themselves and prioritize their workload. "If you're stressed, the patient is going to know you're stressed, and that's not good," Tom Hottman explained. "If you're worried, it may affect your performance. That's not good. So the training offers strategies for taking care of yourself."

When new hires come into Sky Lakes, they are given a condensed version of the training program. It's done over a shorter period of time and taught by employee peers. SEAs get new employees up to speed quickly. Tom believes that the hospital's peer-to-peer training means greater buy-in for both the trainers and the new staff members. "If your manager is teaching you, you might be tempted to say, 'Yes, sir,' because it's your manager saying it. Inside, you may think to yourself, 'Baloney!' When it comes from somebody who is at the same level as you, it has a little bit tighter connection to reality. That's not to say that it's universally accepted, but it's more widely accepted than if it were given to them from 'on high.'"

Once a month, SEAs are invited to lunch with Paul Stewart. It's an empowering experience. "You can ask him anything," Jason said, "and it's a safe environment where it won't come back to get you. He has been amazingly candid. From the lunches, we started taking notes and minutes and distributing them housewide. The directors have told us that the information we're getting from Mr. Stewart is the same that he's giving to them at the directors' meetings. There are no secrets. There are no hidden agendas. He's a good person. He wants everyone to do well. It's not just how good the hospital is doing; he wants everyone to be as happy as she can be and do as good a job as possible. He conveys that well and makes it feel safe to ask questions."

MAKE IT THE STATUS QUO TO REINFORCE WHAT'S RIGHT

"Reinforce what's right" is a mindset that Tom Hottman is happy to see the staff embrace. On one occasion, a front-line employee took it upon himself to reinforce what's right with a coworker. "He went to another individual with whom he was working at the time, but who was not performing as this guy thought he should," Tom recalled. "It's important to praise in public, but to coach and criticize in private, so he took this employee aside and told him, 'This is not the way we do things. This is not who we are.' Peer to peer! That's powerful stuff. We even terminated some employees because they seemed to be unwilling to accept the changing culture. That was a huge rock in a small pond. The ripples went out. We're serious about this. We're elevating our higher performers so that they can do more, and putting lower performers on notice that their behavior is not going to be tolerated."

HAVE SERVICE RECOVERY TOOLS AND KNOW HOW TO USE THEM

Front-line employees are trained and trusted to use service recovery tools, which include gift certificates to restaurants, stores, gas stations, and movie theaters, as well as a variety of other offerings. These items are available for smoothing out situations where patients have to wait or a mistake is made.

"There is a process in learning how to deal with complaints," Jason Card shared. "We tend to chuckle because Brian Lee tends to come up with things that rhyme: 'Whoever hears a complaint becomes the customer's saint.' Basically, what it means is, not only listen to the person who complains, but actually listen to what she says. Validate what she is saying by writing it down. If you can't help her, find somebody who can. Don't let the issue drop until you have either handed it to somebody who has agreed to carry on with it or brought some satisfaction to the family."

Sky Lakes staff members are taught to listen to the patient's concern and acknowledge the issue, whether they personally think it's an issue or not. If a customer brings it up, it's an issue. "Listen," Tom Hottman advises. "You will learn the answers. You will learn the questions, if you just listen."

Patients are always thanked and validated for bringing up a complaint. "We've been trying to instill in our people that you can treat a complaint in one of two ways," Jason Card explained. "You can be ticked off about it, or you can look at it as a gift, because that person has identified something in your system that doesn't work quite right. It gives you the opportunity to fix it, because it's not affecting just one person, it's affecting the ten people it happened to before and the hundred people it would happen to after. Bringing it to our attention really is a gift to us to help us improve. If we haven't satisfied someone, then as a last resort we have service recovery toolboxes in every department on every floor."

"When you mess up, you 'fess up and dress up," Brian Lee added. "Dressing up works 95 percent of the time. It means saying, 'I apologize.' The other 5 percent of the time, there also needs to be some atonement. You need to do something special."

Tom Hottman points the way to wisdom by posing a question. "What did your mom teach you?" he asked. "You say you're sorry and you mean it. Lately, saying you're sorry has become just words. Instead of just saying it, we show it. We have empowered employees who have tools so that they can say, 'I'm really sorry we made you wait so long. That's not how we normally do things. You're going to be getting your procedure pretty soon, but here is a gift card to a local department store. Take this as a sign of my apology.'" Front-line employees are empowered to decide for themselves when an atonement gift is appropriate. After all, Sky Lakes managers can't be familiar with every situation, and they are busy with other responsibilities.

The service recovery toolbox is also available to demonstrate human compassion. Being able to give a child a teddy bear or a family a gift of flowers can be the most appropriate and profound action to offer comfort to patients.

The skills for using customer service tools are reinforced during peer-to-peer training with instruction, role-playing, and discussions. Jason Card teaches his front-line staff, "If someone drove 40 miles to get here and a scheduling error occurs, we say, 'We are going to track down why this happened and try to make sure it doesn't happen again.' We'll talk to the person who scheduled it. We'll talk to the doctor to see what happened to him. If she's available, we'll even have the supervisor of the department come out and talk to the person and explain what's going on. We might also give him a $40 gas card to let him know that we are sorry, we appreciate that he made the effort to be here, and it was our fault that he can't have the procedure done."

"I wish we could say we were completely successful, but wait times continue to be an issue in different areas of the organization," Tom Hottman noted. "There are so many things we can't control. We are getting better. There is something in trying to turn the enterprise. We have to be patient."

Tom encourages everyone with the phrase, "Fix the problem, not the blame," he said. "We're still human. It's hard to get past wanting to blame someone. We need to fix the problem with procedures, with coaching, and by looking at what caused the problem in the first place. We aren't perfect, but by and large we do a very good job."

Making himself available to staff members is something that Tom makes sure to do as reinforcement for use of the service recovery tools. "He's more than willing to talk to you," Jason shared. "He's the contact person. He's the head of the program, and he's ridiculously busy but fully committed and on board. He's done a wonderful job."

SCRIPTS ARE A STARTING POINT FOR IMPROVING THE CUSTOMER'S EXPERIENCE

The more Sky Lakes works the tools, the more the tools work. Jason and many other members of the front-line staff have noticed a difference in their awareness of why they do what they do, and the positive results that ensue. "Every time I go out in the lobby to get a patient, it's different from the way I did it three years ago," Jason noted. "It's not necessarily different in terms of treating patients better or worse, but making an effort to talk to them and see how they are doing. Making an effort to see how registration went for them. If they had an issue, I take a second to stop, write it down, and say, 'Okay, let me look into that and I'll get back to you.' It's more a consciousness of going the extra mile to give the best service possible."

Scripting is tailored as a starting place for ideas that hospital staff members want to get across to patients. "In our department, we've tried to help registration identify some areas where people might be able to improve their customer feedback," he explained. Scripts were created at a DO IT meeting and offered as an example of what could be said. This allows the employees to personalize their responses to patients so that they can express what needs to be said in a natural way, making it their own.

"For a while, we had patients who didn't feel that we were respecting their privacy. So for me personally, instead of saying, 'I need you to take off everything from the waist up and put this gown on. I'll step out and give you a couple of minutes,' I just added the words, 'I'm going to shut the curtain for your privacy. If you need anything, I'll be on the other side. Just feel free to call.'"

Inserting the word *privacy* into the message is a subtle change that made a big difference. "Even though we were thinking of people's privacy before, now we're actually telling them that we are thinking of their privacy," Jason explained. "There are varying levels of scripting, but that's what it is."

During a service recovery situation, there are certain scripts that employees go through to make sure they follow procedures without missing anything. "If you don't go through the steps—listen to what they say, acknowledge them, and validate them—but jump immediately to the service recovery toolbox and give them some movie tickets, they are going to be offended. They'll feel like you're trying to buy them off," Jason said.

"People find themselves using these skills in their personal lives, too. The funny thing is, we've got several couples that work in the organization who are either consciously or subconsciously using the tools they learned for conflict resolution with their spouses. They're like, 'Wait a minute, I remember that from the workshop!' Once you've been doing it for so long, it becomes a part of you and crosses over into your personal life."

ACKNOWLEDGING EXCELLENCE BRINGS MORE EXCELLENCE

The third cornerstone of the culture change that CLS brought to Sky Lakes is called Execution Excellence. In many ways, from the execution of a polite greeting to compassionately executing effective service recovery, the Sky Lakes staff embraced this call for excellence. To reinforce Execution Excellence, Sky Lakes created empowering ways to acknowledge and appreciate staff members. One example is the Excellence Patrol, a process that allows anyone to report a staff member who has made a difference. "You can call a number, and Tom Hottman and a couple of other people on the committee use a phone tree to get five or six people together," Jason explained. "They go as soon as they can after the service has happened to say on the spot, 'We saw what you did, and we really appreciate the difference you made.' The person's manager or supervisor will try to come with us. It takes maybe five minutes." The person being acknowledged receives a balloon, a giant chocolate bar in a custom "Sky Lakes Service Excellence" wrapper, and a thank-you card from the CEO.

One of the Excellence Patrols in which Jason participated involved a family that had been traveling through the area when the pregnant wife went into labor unexpectedly. They came to Sky Lakes and had to adjust to the fact that they would not be able to have their child delivered by their own doctor in their own hospital. Since it was over the weekend, the staff members who generally do discharges were not available.

"These people were happy to have the baby, but they wanted to get home as soon as possible," Jason shared. "We had a lady from medical records who came in from home on a Saturday night to go through the process and make sure the paperwork was done so that these people could take their new baby home on Sunday morning. This goes to show that there is no weak link in the system. It's not just about the doctors and nurses and the people who take physical care of patients. This staff member obviously deserved recognition from us, but the people wrote a beautiful letter thanking the hospital for the wonderful care that they had. I think that by that one selfless act, she made all the difference for those people."

Someone from her department reported what she had done over the weekend. "We all came, and our CEO Paul Stewart told her, 'This is the kind of thing that validates our service excellence teachings, but also, it's people like you doing things like this that make us the provider of choice. It shows people that we're here to provide the best possible care that we can and help us achieve our mission statement.' Paul himself was the one who handed her the balloon and the candy. We all shook her hand in front of her peers and in front of her manager and director. That is just one example. There are countless others."

"BE NICE" IS A CRITICAL MANDATE

When asked for an example of another key practice embraced by Sky Lakes, Tom said, "'Be nice.' Being nice should be fairly easy, particularly for people whose job it is to take care of people."

Sky Lakes is a large hospital, and it's easy to get lost in its corridors if you've never been there. While the patient care area is in the new part of the hospital, the MRI, x-ray, and test lab departments are in the old building. It can be confusing for patients trying to make their way through the new building to the old.

"The instructions are 'Take, don't tell,'" Tom explained. "We escort anyone who looks confused or asks for directions. So with that in mind, we had a visitor, Dennis Heck, a marvelous man from Custom Learning Systems and a former hospital CEO, who came in for our annual Service Excellence performance review. He was due to be in the front lobby around seven o'clock in the morning. The sly dog showed up at 6:45 a.m. He's a distinguished-looking man carrying his briefcase, and he went into the lobby and just stood there. Five individuals, five different times, unrelated and unknown to the others, stopped and asked, 'You look like you're looking for something. Can I help you? I can take you there.' It was validation of the progress that had been made. When Dennis Heck, a guy with a world of knowledge says, 'I was impressed,' my day is made."

It is remarkable to see the lengths to which Sky Lakes goes to provide exquisite service. "We take care of people," Tom stated. "We didn't launch Service Excellence to improve our patient satisfaction scores, although that is a result. We did not do it because it was going to improve our market share and our bottom line, although our market share is up. Those are all by-products. We did it because it was the right thing to do."

* * *

Now that you've read the case study for Sky Lakes, it's your turn to be relentless in your pursuit of better customer service at your place of business. By making continuous improvement a normal part of your job, you will gain excellence mastery that will translate into every area of your life. Read through the Practical Points, Progress Checklist, and Lessons Learned sections that follow and notice which ideas you are already putting to use in your own business and which ones you can adopt. Then set a goal to improve how you serve your customers.

PRACTICAL POINTS

Point 1: Customer service is about cultivating a culture of inclusivity.

Sky Lakes extends inclusivity to its definition of a customer when it describes its customers as both patients and families. Understand the sense of peace that comes from having emotional support and the value that comes from working together. Inclusivity creates cohesiveness. Companywide engagement and accountability create a culture of inclusivity. Those who are not part of the solution become part of the problem. When everyone in management is put on a team to implement a customer service best practice and is expected to report back to his peers, the level of accountability improves, and so do the results.

Point 2: Customer service is about seeing every complaint as a gift.

Complaining customers are willing to tell you what others will not. Research reveals that 90 percent of unhappy customers won't tell you that they are dissatisfied. In all probability, you've been one of those 90 percent. Why would dissatisfied customers choose to stay silent? Perhaps they're not comfortable with how their complaint will be addressed. Perhaps they aren't emotionally connected enough with your company to care. When you view a complaint as a gift to help your company improve, your compassionate response can set things right and improve the customer relationship. CLS supplied Sky Lakes with the following facts: Only one out of 26 customers will bother to complain. A happy customer will tell five others; an unhappy customer will tell ten others. It costs five times as much to create a new customer as it does to keep an existing one satisfied. Respond to your customers' complaints within 24 to 48 hours and 95 percent will stay with you.

Point 3: Customer service is about educating and empowering the front line.

Select your top-performing front-line staff members and train them to train their peers. When the front line sees someone on their own level who is excited and enthusiastic about the customer service program, it's more infectious than hearing it from management. Empower those on the front line by trusting them to make on-the-spot service recovery decisions without having to go to a manager for approval.

Point 4: Customer service is about ongoing implementation.

Track your customers' primary dissatisfiers by charting their complaints for follow-up and using measurement tools to gauge customer satisfaction. Create constant, ongoing processes that address those dissatisfiers. Shift the perception that improvement efforts are something that happens occasionally by making improvement a part of everyone's job description.

Point 5: Customer service is about the inspired use of service recovery tools.

The way you handle service recovery can endear your company to customers, making them more loyal than they were before. Before jumping to a solution, take the time to fully listen to and acknowledge the customer. Give a genuine apology, and let her know how you plan to follow up so that a similar situation is not likely to happen again. Being heard and understood is sometimes all it takes, but at other times you need to make atonement. Give the customer something more than he expected. Sky Lakes has a service recovery kit in virtually every department, on each floor of the hospital, to help the staff members offer something extra to customers when issues arise that are outside of their control.

Point 6: Customer service is about showing appreciation.

Appreciate your staff and coworkers for simple acts of kindness as well as exquisite acts of over-the-top customer service. What you focus on expands. Sky Lakes has an Excellence Patrol to give on-the-spot acknowledgement in a quick, yet powerful way. Fellow coworkers report exceptional acts of customer service, and the staff member is publicly appreciated by management, his supervisor, and his coworkers.

Point 7: Customer service is about being nice.

The price of being "not nice" is too high to ignore, especially in today's global economy. Sky Lakes put procedures in place to make "being nice" an actionable part of the company culture. "Take, don't tell" is an example of putting being nice into action by giving customers the courtesy of taking them to their destination, instead of simply telling them how to get there. When someone is nice, good feelings and a natural attraction keep customers connected to your company.

PROGRESS CHECKLIST

As you read the following checklist, rate yourself on a scale from one to ten. How skilled are you at applying the lessons learned from Sky Lakes Medical Center and Custom Learning Systems? What inspired actions can you take today to get into a mindset of continuous improvement?

1-2-3-4-5-6-7-8-9-10

_____ Cultivate a culture of inclusivity.
_____ See every complaint as a gift.
_____ Educate and empower front-line staff.
_____ Implement customer service best practices continuously.
_____ Use service recovery tools.
_____ Appreciate employees for what they're doing right.
_____ Be nice.

LESSONS LEARNED

The story of Sky Lakes Medical Center shows how a genuine desire to help customers, combined with effective tools, can raise the level of customer satisfaction. The relentless pursuit of continuous improvement offers a myriad of added benefits. It increases revenues, helps retain excellent staff, and enhances the perception of your company in your community. To gain access to these engaging skills and make them a part of your everyday practice, read through the following questions. Answer each one for yourself before reading our responses to notice how well you understand the concepts.

1. What can be done to encourage a shy employee to use the six-foot rule?

_____
_____
_____
_____
_____

2. How do you motivate employees to provide service excellence?

_____
_____
_____
_____
_____

3. How can you ensure that front-line staff members take advantage of service recovery tools?

_____
_____
_____
_____
_____

4. What can you do to reduce the number of low performers at your company?

_____
_____
_____
_____
_____

5. What can you do to stay positive when a cantankerous customer is pressing your buttons?

_____
_____
_____
_____
_____

6. What happens when some members of the management team are disengaged from the customer service initiatives?

_____
_____
_____
_____
_____

7. Are there any other effective uses for service recovery tools?

_____
_____
_____
_____
_____

ANSWERS

1. **What can be done to encourage a shy employee to use the six-foot rule?**

    It can take a bit of encouragement and time for shy employees to get comfortable making eye contact with and offering a verbal greeting to absolutely anyone coming within six feet of them. Keep the expectation and offer private coaching to the shy employee, noting his progress and growing ease. With practice, the new behavior will become second nature to him.

2. **How do you motivate employees to provide service excellence?**

    Encourage employees to self-regulate. You can inspire them by helping them connect to the emotional aspects of why they do their job and why they chose to be in the service profession in the first place. Pose questions and listen while your people come to conclusions themselves, rather than relying on external reasons. Have meetings where ideas can be shared and consensus can be built so that the service tools are owned by all.

3. **How can you ensure that front-line staff members take advantage of service recovery tools?**

    When employees understand and have compassion for their customers, they typically have a natural desire to aid them. Training is essential. People don't know what they don't know. Looking at situations from the customer's point of view can be reinforced in workshops through role-playing and conversation. To reinforce the correct use of service recovery tools like gift cards and movie passes, set up regular meetings to share stories and examples. Document the results of service recovery. Typically, customers become more bonded with your organization, in spite of something that may have gone wrong, because of how service recovery was handled. Review service recovery incidents in meetings with your staff in order to figure out the reason why something went wrong so that it can be fixed. Regular and consistent employee communication through e-mails, posting of flyers, and regularly scheduled meetings is a requirement for a strong service recovery effort.

4. **What can you do to reduce the number of low performers at your company?**

If you continually reinforce your expectations to your staff, you will easily recognize those employees who are not living up to the standards that have been set. Elevate your high performers. Encourage peer-to-peer training to deepen the level of commitment and employee buy-in. At job interviews, ask and record what candidates say about their commitment to service excellence, and then use those comments as a point of reference during performance reviews. When low performers work with an empowered front line, they become uncomfortable. People like working with people who have the same work ethic and expectations. Make it clear that low performers will not be tolerated. Further, by investing in high performers, you are preparing them to be future managers who will be able to perpetuate a culture of excellence.

5. **What can you do to stay positive when a cantankerous customer is pressing your buttons?**

When you feel stressed dealing with a challenging customer, realize that your feelings have nothing to do with what the customer is "doing to you" and everything to do with your skills. Sky Lakes provided a Dealing with Difficult People workshop for its staff. Customers do what they do and say what they say when they are upset. Take a few deep breaths. Connect to your body and remind yourself, "This isn't personal." Role-play with coworkers after the fact to find better ways of handling recurring situations that most trigger your stress.

6. **What happens when some members of the management team are disengaged from the customer service initiatives?**

Disengagement and failure to follow up can kill your customer service initiatives. Some leaders are fully engaged; some may not be. Brian Lee of Custom Learning Systems said, "Every leader must be engaged in being part of the solution, or she is part of the problem. If you look at most organizations that attempt major initiatives, what they do is set up a task force or performance team. Basically, it's a quality improvement team, and it might have a hundred leaders, eight of whom are involved. Though they are pretty committed, the other ninety-two are saying, 'I've told these guys they aren't doing it right.' Those ninety-two people who aren't involved are the problem." Requiring every member of the leadership team to stay actively involved, the way Sky Lakes did with OASIS teams, adds accountability so that you can keep the customer service improvement momentum going.

7. **Are there any other effective uses for service recovery tools?**

At Sky Lakes, front-line employees are given the freedom to determine if a simple act of compassion is appropriate. That might mean purchasing flowers, a toy, or some other token as an expression of care for a patient. When the members of your service staff are tapped into their true purpose for serving, they will inevitably develop instincts about when to offer something extra to comfort or delight a customer.

WHO'S YOUR GLADYS?

Do you encounter customers who can't find their way? When you are tempted to tell them where to go, don't do it. Personally take them to their destination. This "take, don't tell" rule gives customers your added attention. It will tame their tensions and result in greater customer loyalty.

CHAPTER 10

Communicore Visual Communications: The Happy Challenge

*Communicore Visual Communications, a television produc-
tion studio in Michigan, has a customer base of highly creative people. The television producers and marketing
executives that use its services work in high-pressure environ-
ments and are completely focused on making their vision for the project come
to life. This sometimes means extremely tight deadlines and high levels of emotion. Since Lori Jo Vest, coauthor of this book, has been managing director of
Communicore since 2003, she's had a bird's-eye view of what it takes to grow
a company in the highly competitive production industry. The company's client
services staff is trained to do whatever it takes to solve any problem that arises
and to keep its cool when managing tense situations. As a result, Communicore
has thrived and expanded, while many of its competitors have struggled. In this
chapter, you'll discover what happened when Lori gave herself and her staff
member a challenge to bring out the best in themselves as well as in Brenda,
a client's crabby new employee.*

Communicore has a long history of building strong customer relationships. Jeff Carter founded the teleproduction facility in 1995 after
working as a freelance cameraman for 10 years. I joined Communicore in
2000, leaving my position as marketing manager at one of the largest
companies in the television production industry in the United States. It
was a risky move, in some of my colleagues' opinions, as I was leaving a
"sure thing" for a small, lesser-known company in a highly competitive
production community. What most people didn't see was Jeff's compas-

sion and integrity and the quality of the company's work, factors that weighed heavily in my decision.

After 15 years in sales, I knew how to develop strong client relationships. I also had several years of staff management experience. Working at Communicore gave me the opportunity to use those skills to improve the existing structure and grow the company. Every enhancement we made was about serving the customer, from fine-tuning production processes to hiring new staff members. In 2008, Communicore was given a tier one contract to manage the video creation for a major automotive manufacturer. Becoming a tier one vendor means that you have been approved by the company's purchasing department as a cost-effective vendor with a high-quality product. It can be a difficult status for a small company to achieve. There are several hurdles to jump, including convincing the client of your company's worthiness through a written presentation with references, work plans, demo material, and detailed information about your business operations. You also typically undergo a face-to-face question-and-answer session with the clients who are making the decision.

In our case, the competing bidders for the contract were some of the most esteemed production studios in our market. This contract had the potential to double our annual sales, and we were told by our client that two of the main factors in its decision were our reputation for integrity and our excellent customer service. At a time when the economy was sputtering and many of our competitors were shrinking, it was a wonderful affirmation of what we had been striving for since I joined the company.

ACT AS THE STEWARD OF THE CLIENT RELATIONSHIP

In customer service, your job is to act as the steward of the customer relationship, meaning that you take the responsibility for the care of your company's customer relationships. Every customer service contact is an opportunity to strengthen that relationship, even when things have gone horribly wrong. In fact, when you or your company makes a mistake, how well you handle it can enhance the relationship you already have with your client.

In the early years of Communicore's history, owner Jeff Carter received a call to handle a video shoot for one of Detroit's "Big Three" automakers. The company CEO was addressing his top managers at a conference, and there would be only one opportunity to get his speech on tape. Jeff assigned one of his best freelance cameramen to manage the shoot. It seemed to go well. Afterwards, the client took the tapes back to the edit suite to start putting the program together.

The editor popped the tapes into a deck and hit the play button. It sounded great, but there was no video image. As it turned out, the record deck had been wired wrong on the shoot, a simple human error. "I remember so well when I first got the call. I felt like someone had punched me. I was devastated," Jeff recalled. "I had hired one of the best shooters in town for the project, and he had made a mistake. I called the producer, who was one of our toughest customers, and told her exactly what had happened and that we would do whatever it took to make it right."

Now what? The client was editing the program at another company, and it was scheduled to go out via satellite to employees around the country the next morning. Communicore editor Dean Saigeon and the motion graphics designer got to work. They created visuals from the executive's PowerPoint presentation and added vehicle images and other flourishes to make it interesting. They worked through the night to create a program that could be broadcast.

"We were very proactive," Jeff explained. "We took ownership of the problem, figured out what went wrong, and told the truth. Then we fixed it at no charge, of course. People were really surprised by the lengths we went to to make things right. This was the first major blowup we'd experienced, the first opportunity to show who we were going to be as a company. What I learned is that it's all about how you handle it. We were rewarded in the end for doing the right thing. Years later, most people don't remember the actual problem, but they remember how we handled it."

HANDLE MISTAKES WITH CARE AND FOLLOW THROUGH

This proactive approach to managing mistakes is evidenced throughout the company's history. Thirteen years later, I was in the hot seat when another error was made, this time by one of our junior staff members.

It was one of the largest projects that our big ad agency client had ever given us: creating Web ads for a new product from a well-known vacuum cleaner manufacturer. Things went smoothly all the way through the process, from the first production meeting to the last shot. At least, that was what we thought, until the call came in about the missing proto-type vacuum cleaner. Why hadn't it arrived back at the client's headquar-ters the week after the shoot? It was one of only a handful of prototypes in existence at the time. During the shoot and subsequent production wrap-up activities, we had had two of them.

On the day of what became known as "the vacuum incident," I had been out at meetings all afternoon. When I arrived back at the office, my business manager recounted the story: "You wouldn't believe what happened when you were out." The producer for the vacuum cleaner Web videos called and asked if we could provide tracking information for the vacuum shipment. As we explored the circumstances, we discovered that a "perfect storm" had led to our client services coordinator neglect-ing to send the prototype vacuum back.

Coincidentally, on the day of the shoot, Communicore's cleaning person had notified me by e-mail that our company vacuum cleaner was broken. I had been insanely busy and hadn't had time to get back to her. When she came in to clean the following weekend, she was delighted to come across a beautiful brand-new vacuum cleaner with the latest fea-tures in a box that was clearly marked "working vacuum." She proceeded to happily vacuum the floors all over our building and at the company next door. She loved it.

The members of the front desk staff found the whole situation rather amusing. After offering a brief explanation to the client, they took the prototype to FedEx and asked to have it boxed and shipped back. Then they dismissed the situation as a minor problem that had been solved.

As our coordinator recounted the story, my heart sank. She had no idea that this particular vacuum cleaner might be needed at locations across the country for use at promotional events, or that the price tag for a prototype could be significant. To her, it was simply a vacuum cleaner.

I immediately sent her off to FedEx to retrieve the package and bring it back so that I could survey the damage. The vacuum was dirty, and some of the coating had worn off the wheels. I asked her to clean up the vacuum *carefully*, take it to a packaging store, and have it packed "like a Ming vase." I instructed her to insure it for $2,500 and ship it overnight, no matter what the cost. I then called the client to convey how incredi-bly embarrassed I was by our mishandling of the prototype. I made no excuses, told her the complete truth, and apologized profusely for the fact that our staff members weren't aware of the value of this particular vacuum cleaner. I also told her that we had changed our plans for shipping the unit and offered to pay for any repairs that might be needed to make things right. Throughout the conversation, I made sure that she understood that the prototype was just as important to me as it was to her. She sounded relieved and told me that she would get back to me the next day to let me know what happened.

The next morning, I still felt that the situation was a bit incomplete, so I added one more element: I wrote up and e-mailed an explanation of exactly what happened, including an offer to cover any financial costs of bringing the prototype back to its original condition. It offered our customer something in writing that she could forward to her superiors and her client if she determined that it would be helpful to do so.

By the time I followed up with her a day or two later, she considered the situation resolved and asked me to bid on a big production for a new client. Whew! We recovered the relationship, and the agency brought several projects through our door after the infamous "vacuum incident."

I think it was our somewhat over-the-top response to the mistake that made things right. We, as a company, took complete responsibility for the mishap. I explained exactly what had occurred in a telephone call and in an e-mail. Most importantly, I apologized, sharing my authentic feelings of embarrassment and concern.

DRAW OUT BETTER SOLUTIONS WITH A CREATIVE APPROACH

Whether it's recovering from a mistake or contributing to a successful outcome, Candice Lazar, Communicore's senior account manager, loves solving client problems—so much so that she's learned to get comfortable on camera. "One day, I actually went home and packed a suitcase full of clothes so that I could 'act' in a commercial for one of my favorite clients," she said. "He was doing political spots, and he needed a few roughs for focus group testing. It was really funny, because when he asked me to do it, he told me that I'd have to go home and change so that I could be a snotty, uptight woman who felt that society owed her something. I was a bit apprehensive, but it was actually kind of fun. I just went with it. It's how we are at Communicore."

In an industry in which creative personalities, high-tech equipment, and tight deadlines come together, innovative problem solving is mandatory. There are so many things that must fall into place to create a great video program or commercial. It feels like every day we're doing something we've never done before.

When we're presented with a challenge, there are always at least two or three different paths we can take to solve it. "Unfortunately, the first solution we think of doesn't always work. A while back, we decided that when we were really perplexed, we had to come up with three possible solutions before we made a decision about how to move forward," Candice explained. "Usually, it's the second or third idea that is the best one, so if you just go with your first thought, it might not be the best solution."

We've also found that when you really "hit the wall" and can't think of an answer, it helps to talk it through with someone who has not been involved in the situation thus far. Such a person brings a fresh approach and may be able to see the solution much faster than those who have been steeped in the problem since it started. By making this a standard procedure when we're stalled, we are able to come up with better options more efficiently.

CONTROL THE QUALITY OF SERVICE BY PUTTING SYSTEMS INTO PLACE

When I first joined Communicore, the procedures aspect of the operation, as in so many small companies, was still developing. The company had grown from two employees to fourteen in just a few years, and while the employees were experienced, there was a need to tighten up the processes. Fortunately, the individual employees were diligent in making sure that clients' materials were mastered and duplicated properly, although human error or technical glitches sometimes crept in and caused issues. In 2004, one particular incident pointed out the need for a standardized quality control (QC) procedure for DVD and videotape copies.

We had hired an experienced and talented freelance editor to work with one of our most important clients, whom I'll call Stewart. This client had brought us projects for a few years, and he trusted us, which meant that he typically sent DVD copies of the programs we edited for him directly to his customer. This time, when he got the DVD after his session with the freelancer, he decided to take a quick look at it on his own computer before he sent it off. It was fortunate that he did so, as the DVD had the audio from his program, but video from a completely different program, from one of the other edit suites that were in use when his DVD was being made.

One of the most basic procedures that all strong editors in our industry follow is the double-checking of the program material on their videotape and disk copies. They actually watch the tape or DVD to make sure that it plays well through the program from start to finish. It was an incredible lack of judgment on the freelance editor's part to neglect to review the DVD before he gave it to the front desk for delivery to the client.

I received the call from Stewart that afternoon, and he was not happy. He had trusted us, and he was upset that the materials that he had promised his client would now be late. His reputation with his client would be adversely affected, although it could have been much worse. Even so, his trust in us had been shattered.

I drove over to Stewart's office and delivered the replacement DVD personally. I apologized and told him that I would get back to him that afternoon with an explanation of what had happened and what we would be doing to ensure that it wouldn't happen again.

The video business is rather complex. If you check one wrong box in the software setup, accidentally plug a cable into the wrong jack, or have a recorder that's malfunctioning, you can end up with a bad tape or disk. While computers are used, the amount of human input into the final product is still significant. With the tight deadlines under which we sometimes work, a staffer in a hurry can easily overlook something. That was what had happened in this case. I called the client, explained that it was human error, and promised that we were implementing a new QC procedure effective immediately. I assured him that this would mean that a second person, someone who had not been involved in the original making of the DVD or videotape copy, would check it for audio and video quality. Stewart thanked me for "our aggressive approach to solving the problem."

We have since fine-tuned our QC processes, and they are reinforced with our employees at our regular staff meetings. The creation of this one procedure also caused us to begin doing some root cause analysis when things go wrong. We now have standard procedures for several of our processes. Detailed instructions are printed out on colorful paper and laminated to create a ring-bound reference booklet (referred to as the

"Technicolor dream book") that is distributed throughout the Communicore facilities. As a result, we have significantly decreased the number of errors that affect our clients. And Stewart? He's still one of our major clients.

TAKE ON THE CHALLENGE OF WARMING UP CUSTOMER RELATIONSHIPS

One of the first new customers I brought in to Communicore in 2001 was a small agency that did advertising for local and regional clients. This agency produced a fair amount of television, and I always made an extra effort to get to know its new staffers to help ensure that the business would stay with our company, in spite of our client's frequent personnel changes.

A few years back, this client hired a new staffer, a woman I'll call Brenda. As I typically did, I called her and asked if she might have a few minutes so that I could stop by and introduce myself. In a suspicious tone, which I interpreted to mean, "What is this woman going to try to sell me?" she reluctantly agreed, and we set up a meeting time a few days later.

When I walked into her space at the agency, she seemed none too happy about my visit. Usually, my 20 years of sales experience meant that I could find a quick common ground with just about any new customer. This time was different. Brenda gave me a quick handshake and the brush-off. "I only have a second," she said, taking my material and almost challenging me to start a conversation. I took the hint, handed her our demo reel and my business card, and made a brief statement about our services. As we walked toward the door, I asked her to please call me if there was anything I could do for her as she adjusted to her new position.

Over the next several months, Brenda called me and our scheduler quite a few times, and she always sounded somewhat angry. When the receptionist told either of us that Brenda was on hold, we'd groan and make a face. "Oh, geez, I wonder what she wants now?" Noticing the difficulty that both of us were having with the conversations, I issued a challenge that I thought might brighten things up and have a positive effect on our new customer. "Let's make it our goal to befriend Brenda. Let's bend over backwards to make sure she knows, without a doubt, that whatever she needs, whenever she needs it, we'll take care of it. Let's be extraordinarily nice to her, no matter how she acts when she calls. And let's make it our goal to be so genuinely friendly to her that eventually she won't be able to help but be friendly back," I suggested. And we did.

When we called Brenda and she virtually barked the name of her agency into the phone, I said, "Hi, Brenda, how are you? This is Lori," in my cheeriest tone. "Just calling to make sure you got the delivery I sent to you this morning. Did it arrive okay?" or maybe, "Of course, Brenda, I would love to get that handled for you. Why don't I send our intern by to pick up your package so you don't have to wait for your courier to get back to the office?" The niceties went on and on, and no matter how crabby Brenda was, the challenge of loosening her up and helping her realize that we were, and always would be, helpful every time actually made it fun.

Slowly, Brenda began to thaw. It took about six months, but she started warming up. She would take a minute to tell me what kind of day she was having and even sounded happy to hear from me. She started telling me about her pets and how she was having a new refrigerator delivered. She told our scheduler about a trip she was taking to Italy. She began acting nicer when she called. Was it ever rewarding! I actually began looking forward to her calls to see if she would be in a good mood.

One of my proudest customer service moments came when Brenda called me to find out how she should handle a problem she was experiencing with one of our competitors. Her boss liked to "spread the wealth" by working with different suppliers, rather than counting on one vendor. Brenda was working with one of our competitors and having difficulty getting a basic request handled. I gave her some great inside perspective so that she'd know what was reasonable and what wasn't. I thanked her for trusting me enough to share that she had to go somewhere else with this particular project, and we hung up. Today, although she still sometimes barks a bit, Brenda is a much more pleasant customer. Thanks to our "happy challenge," even though we know that she's never going to turn into a totally friendly person, at least she's nicer to us.

KNOW WHEN TO SAY GOOD-BYE

Unfortunately, some unfriendly customers do not improve their behavior, no matter how well you treat them. We experienced this in the early 2000s when we began working with the owner of a great franchise restaurant concept that started in metro Detroit in the mid-1990s. It was created by a curmudgeonly man whom I'll refer to as Oscar. The franchise was getting popular and growing quickly when Communicore began working with him through his ad agencies to create commercials.

Unfortunately, Oscar chose his advertising agencies based on price, and most of the work that was done for him was low-end and less than stellar. We were appalled by the footage the agencies would bring us, although we'd do our best to create a workable spot for him.

Over time, we had built up quite a library of Oscar's commercials in our videotape library. His media buyer, the person who buys the airtime from the television stations and gets the copies of the spots to them, would call us, order this or that commercial, and tell us where to send it. The ad agencies continued to change, seemingly with every commercial, and the spots continued to be based on cheap ideas and low-budget, low-quality production techniques.

Communicore and our audio neighbors, RMS Studios, continued to work with Oscar for three or four years, doing the best we could with what he brought in. We struggled with Oscar's inability to keep track of his tapes and graphic elements, which he sometimes took with him at the end of his edit sessions. While we had meticulous records of the tapes that we had sent out, he never seemed to know where the items he had checked out had gone. It was a great affirmation of our record keeping, as we had sign-out sheets for all the items he had taken with him.

One day, Oscar called and said that he needed to see "everything," all of his tapes and commercial masters, because he wanted to sort through them to locate one of his older TV commercials. I set up a time for him to come in, put all the tapes in a bin, and asked him to let us know what he would be taking with him so that we could prepare the proper sign-out records. There were at least 40 tapes, so I left him in the tape library with the boxes of his materials. A few minutes later, he asked, "Do you have a bag?" and I provided him with one, assuming that he would pack up what he needed, and then before he left we could prepare the list. It wasn't until half an hour had passed that I realized that Oscar had walked out the door with all of his materials and left us with no way to confirm what he had taken.

"Great," I thought. I asked our client services coordinator to print out two copies of the list of materials with a place for Oscar's signature, wrote a polite letter explaining why we were requesting his signature on the enclosed list, and put one in the mail to him with a self-addressed, stamped envelope. I figured, let's make it as easy as possible for him to complete this simple task. I kept one copy for my own files with a copy of the letter and a brief note stating what had happened. Then, just to cover all my bases, I left him a voice mail message, suggesting that perhaps he had forgotten to review the materials with us and that I'd "so appreciate it" if he'd sign off on the tapes he had taken so that we could maintain our accurate library records. I called again a few weeks later, and when I reached him, he indignantly claimed, "They're my tapes, so I don't have to sign anything!"

The best part? I didn't take any of his actions personally. Oscar was an unusually cranky customer who simply decided to do something that didn't follow Communicore's procedures. The most I could do was attempt to rectify the situation to the best of my ability, make sure we had a written record of what had happened, and then let it go. (Good records are a requirement in a situation like this one, in case they're ever needed for legal purposes.)

Did I ever hear from Oscar after he snuck out of Communicore with all of his tapes? Of course. Several months later, he called to get a commercial dubbed for airing on one of the local network affiliate stations. Did we have it? No. Did we have a record of what happened to it? Yes, but with no signature, it wasn't as strong as I'd have liked. I explained the situation to him and, fortunately, that was that. I discussed the circumstances within our client services staff, and we decided that we would not accept any further business from this particular client. Fortunately, we've not had to officially "fire" him, something we've always tried to avoid.

Unfortunately, not all client conflicts can be resolved. While Communicore has a large stable of loyal clients, there have been a few customers, besides Oscar, who presented issues that couldn't be resolved. In a few cases, the "wear and tear" on our team members conflicted with Communicore's culture of valuing clients, team members, and vendors. Whether because of a client's outrageous demands or because of inappropriate behavior, the management team has sometimes decided to discontinue a client relationship. However, even then, the offending client is treated with respect, and the transition to the new production facility is handled professionally by our entire staff.

KNOW WHEN A CUSTOMER IS NOT A FIT AND ATTRACT THOSE THAT ARE

In 2001, the World Trade Center bombing hit the American economy, causing sales to decline at most companies, including Communicore. The economic climate in metro Detroit was uncertain; clients had less money to spend, and our sales slowed down significantly. Times were tough, so when a potential client called to talk to us about a campaign of animated commercials, we were definitely interested in talking to him. He talked a good game, offering all kinds of stories about his connections in the business. He claimed to be in search of a series of 3D animated commercials, with a production budget that was fully funded. But there was something about this man that was disturbing. "He came through hustling," Jeff recalled. "It was post 9/11 and we were a bit desperate, but something didn't feel right." We met with him, discussing all the specifications for the project and running the budgets in our heads. We were skeptical, but we weren't sure exactly why.

"Do you think this guy actually has any funding?" I asked Jeff. Neither of us was convinced, but the possibilities were enticing. I wandered back to my office after the man left, feeling a strong urge to wash my hands, yet I couldn't quite put my finger on what it was about this prospect that was so disquieting.

Just as he left, our 3D animator, who had been in the meeting with us and who would serve as lead on the project, came up front and stopped by my office. This well-funded, highly connected client with the big 3D project had stopped by our graphics department on the way out and solicited our animator to work for him on the side.

"We politely declined the work and offered him the phone numbers of some of our competitors," Jeff shared. "It was easy to turn down the bid. We had already learned to follow our instincts and use that internal sense of judgment. It saved us time and effort in the end, I'm sure.

"We continually ask ourselves, 'What did we learn?' whenever things veer off course. Those times give us the opportunity to prove our integrity and gain the trust of our employees, our clients, and our vendors," he added. "As an owner, I have to be the type of person that I want to attract. If I didn't run the business a certain way, I wouldn't have been able to attract the type of people that I have working here. The people who have come along and been attracted to working here have been quality people.

"It applies to the customers, too. Of course, there's more wiggle room with clients, because it's not a perfect world. We have to have a bit more tolerance. But it's great when you attract customers who live by similar principles. I want this place [Communicore] to be a blessing to our employees, and the same for our vendors and our customers."

Jeff also believes that a challenging business climate can be a time of great growth and learning for any company. "It forces you to be disciplined in spending and equipment purchases. If you continue to transform your company and make it better, be creative, and work with integrity, you end up loving where you are."

* * *

Now that you've read the case study for Communicore Visual Communications, how can you take a creative problem-solving approach to serving your clients? Read through the Practical Points, Progress Checklist, and Lessons Learned sections that follow and notice which ideas you are already putting to use in your own business and which ones you can adopt. Then set a goal of coming up with new ideas for handling customer service challenges and operational issues.

PRACTICAL POINTS

Point 1: Honesty truly is the best policy.

No one wants to look bad to a client, particularly if the mistake was one that could easily have been avoided. However, everyone can appreciate the fact that people make mistakes. Honesty is the best approach, even if you or someone on your staff has made a serious mistake. Customers appreciate knowing the truth, and telling it proves your integrity. Plus, once you admit what happened down to the smallest detail, you can set about making things right.

Point 2: Taking complete responsibility leads to a speedy recovery.

Take responsibility for making sure that every customer transaction in which you are involved ends with a happy customer. This applies particularly for those occasions that are headed south at 250 miles an hour. If you make a commitment to personally correct anything that has gone wrong, your efforts can not only save the client relationship, but strengthen it, as the client sees how dedicated you are to setting things right.

Point 3: Treat every customer interaction as an opportunity to strengthen the relationship.

If you're in the middle of a crazy afternoon and the phone rings with a customer's immediate request, it's easy to rush through the call with too much efficiency, missing an opportunity to connect. In reality, it takes only about 30 seconds to ask someone how her day is going and throw a few sentences of pleasant banter into a telephone conversation. Give a little bit more than your client expects, whether that means following up to make sure that he received his shipment or sending along a magazine article about something that interests him. It can make a world of difference to the customer relationship.

Point 4: Use both your heart and your head.

Developing your customer service skills can be a confusing proposition. You're told to develop a relationship with the customer. "Make it personal," the experts say. "Make a heartfelt connection with her so that she comes back." Then, in the next article you read, they say, "Don't take customer conflicts personally." How can you use your heart and your head at the same time?

Actually, it's easy. It's personal when things are going well. When the customer first walks into your establishment or calls you on the telephone, it's personal. You're developing a relationship that you hope will be stronger than the customer's connection to your competitors. You smile, pay complete attention to him, and do your best to ascertain his every need and fill it. You ask about his pets, his kids, his favorite sports team—but only if he seems open to taking the conversation to a more personal level. People like to do business with people they like, and one of the most important aspects of being a great customer service rep is the ability to connect with customers.

It's not personal when there is a problem. When the customer doesn't get her delivery on time or when there's a mistake in the order or when she's just having a bad day, that's when you respond 100 percent from your head. That's when you're representing the company, not yourself, in the transaction. When you're resolving a customer service issue, adding your own emotions (anxiety, irritation, anger) to the mix is a big fat *no-no*. That's when you need to think the most clearly so that you can use your best creative problem-solving skills. When your customers know that they can count on you to be friendly, responsive, and cordial—no matter what is happening—it strengthens the relationship.

Point 5: Take action to solve each problem you discover.

What if you were the front-line responder to every customer who comes in angry because the coffee lid on the coffee that you're serving came off, and coffee spilled in the customer's lap? Would you continue to serve the coffee with the same lids, hour after hour, while one customer after another came in and yelled at you? Of course not. You'd take action (tell your boss, order different lids, whatever it took) and change the circumstances. What if you took action on even the smallest recurring problems that you have at your place of business, even if they aren't quite as extreme as this example? When you uncover the cause of a problem that affects your customers, taking responsibility for fixing it will ensure that it doesn't become a recurring issue that drives away business.

Point 6: Find joy in turning around negative customer interactions.

Some customers will be more challenging than others. Their life experiences may have taught them that they won't get what they need unless they're aggressive. They may be struggling with something in their personal life that is causing them to behave poorly toward the people around them. Whatever it is, you can maintain your positive demeanor by issuing a "happy challenge" to yourself. Whenever you speak to a crabby customer, be a little extra friendly and helpful. Go overboard with positive energy, and don't let his mood affect yours. In most cases, even if the customer doesn't ever become as happy and positive as you are, he may become less negative in his interactions with you as he learns to trust you. While it may seem like you're making extra effort for someone who doesn't deserve the attention, the payoff can be huge.

Point 7: Know when to say good-bye.

Understand that not every customer will be a good fit for your business. Clients who repeatedly act inappropriately toward you or your staff members, or who refuse to follow the necessary processes that allow you to do a good job for them, may need to be removed from your client list. In many cases, doing business is a two-way street, requiring certain behavior from both the customer and the vendor. Don't let a customer's negative demeanor or lack of integrity adversely affect your business. Politely encourage such customers to move on to your competitors. An explanation as simple as, "Our business relationship is not a good fit for either of us" can keep the customer relationship respectful, even when it's ending.

PROGRESS CHECKLIST

As you read the following checklist, rate yourself on a scale from one to ten. How well are you applying the lessons learned from Communicore? What can you do today to get creative and increase your scores in each category?

1-2-3-4-5-6-7-8-9-10

_____ Be honest.

_____ Take complete responsibility for a speedy recovery.

_____ Strengthen the relationship with every interaction.

_____ Use both your heart and your head.

_____ Take action when you discover a problem.

_____ Find joy in turning around negative customer interactions.

_____ Know when to say good-bye.

LESSONS LEARNED

The story of Lori Jo Vest, Jeff Carter, and the staff at Communicore reveals eye-opening ways to solve problems with maximum creativity. To help you apply these skills in your workplace, read through the following questions. Answer each one for yourself before reading our responses to see how many creative ideas you can generate.

1.   Why is it important to get acquainted with the new staffers of your business-to-business customers?

_____

_____

_____

_____

_____

2.   How can you find a genuine way of being friendly when the customer acts hostile, rude, or cold?

_____

_____

_____

_____

3. How do you respond when you discover that your customer is also doing business with your competitors?

_____

_____

_____

_____

_____

4. How do you handle a customer who refuses to follow your company's protocols?

_____

_____

_____

_____

5. When is the best time to review the question, "What did we learn?"

_____

_____

_____

_____

6. What are the pitfalls that might tempt you not to act with integrity when dealing with customers?

_____

_____

_____

_____

7. How do you make your company attractive to the type of employees, vendors, and customers that you most want to work with?

_____

_____

_____

_____

_____

ANSWERS

1. **Why is it important to get acquainted with the new staffers of your business-to-business customers?**

   By reaching out to new employees and offering them your assistance, you can begin forming a positive relationship. Informing them about the services your company offers to their new employer is a good place to start. While new employees sometimes bring preferred vendors from their previous job with them, you can lessen the chances of losing business by being proactive.

2. **How can you find a genuine way of being friendly when the customer acts hostile, rude, or cold?**

   If you keep the big picture in mind and consider yourself the steward of the client relationship, you will behave in a way that supports that end result. You can also create a "happy challenge" that keeps you focused on your goal of ensuring that every customer interaction ends on a positive note.

3. **How do you respond when you discover that your customer is also doing business with your competitors?**

   Your customers may not always work with, or purchase from, your company. Sometimes a customer will choose your competitor for reasons that are beyond your control. The customer may like the people there or want to "spread the wealth." If you continue to serve such customers at the highest levels, you will most likely continue to get business from them. However, if you react negatively, you are essentially negating the client's judgment of what serves him best, and that is never good for the customer relationship.

4. **How do you handle a customer who refuses to follow your company's protocols?**

   The best way to deal with customers who won't follow the procedures you've set up to help you serve them (like credit applications, paperwork, or approval signatures) is to remind them, persuade them, and redirect them in a patient manner. Most clients will eventually understand that your processes help you ensure a high-quality product or experience and will come around to doing what needs to be done. If they don't, you may wish to reconsider the relationship, particularly if it's adversely affecting your staff.

5. **When is the best time to review the question, "What did we learn?"**

    When things go wrong, a quick postmortem analysis, performed while there's still a bit of a "sting" to the situation, can help you avoid a recurrence of the problem. However, if such an analysis is not done immediately, it loses its impact, as staff members may forget important details or lose their strong desire to solve the problem. Getting to the root of the problem may take only a few minutes, yet it can pay off in long-term benefits.

6. **What are the pitfalls that might tempt you not to act with integrity when dealing with customers?**

    Many service providers struggle with being truthful at all times for several reasons. Sometimes the truth isn't what the customer wants to hear, or you may wish to avoid being chastised by your boss. Remember that truth builds trust and that being untruthful will inevitably have a negative impact on a relationship.

7. **How do you make your company attractive to the type of employees, vendors, and customers that you most want to work with?**

    Gandhi said, "You must be the change you wish to see in the world." At Communicore, Jeff Carter's belief in providing the highest possible levels of quality and integrity has proved to be very attractive to customers, employees, and vendors that appreciate those principles. When you set high standards for both your product and your behavior, you will notice that you naturally attract customers, vendors, and employees who share your values.

WHO'S YOUR GLADYS?

Does her very name evoke a groan from your staff? What would happen if you issued a happy challenge and made each interaction with her a "happy to see you" kind of experience? It took Lori's client, Brenda, six months to thaw, but in the end, she became a much more pleasant patron. As you take this creative approach to problem solving, don't be surprised if you experience more fun in your work and easier-to-manage customers.

CHAPTER 11

A Final Review

Now that you've read the intimate details of the customer service practices of 10 successful companies, you've learned new tactics and tools that you can use to keep customers— even the most difficult ones—coming back. Now it's time to set your own course for success. This last chapter will help you take action so that you can provide the best possible service to your Gladys and all of your customers. We've provided a brief summary of each facet of customer service excellence, accompanied by exercises to help you develop your own unique approach.

GLADYS RESPONDS WHEN YOU PAY ATTENTION TO DETAILS

"Beware of the man who won't be bothered with details."
—William Feather

The people at Professional Movers are true masters of excellent customer service. They spend time with their new customers up front, asking questions and taking notes. By the time their crew shows up on the day of the move, its members have been briefed and are ready to cater to each person's unique needs.

Professional Movers also knows how to "love up the unlovable" by developing a positive relationship with even its crankiest clientele. The company's attention to detail turns vocal critics like Gladys into loyal fans who love referring business to it.

How can you learn more about your customers' unique needs? When you first start doing business with someone, take the time to ask him a lot of questions with a sense of curiosity. Ask him what he wants, then listen closely to his responses. Take notes and pass along the information to the employees that will be working with that customer.

Make an effort to truly get to know your clients. You can develop strong client relationships by showing a genuine interest in your customers as people. Pay attention to each customer, even when she's unpleasant. Letting an angry customer vent allows her to get the negative feelings out of her system, so that you can get the relationship back on track.

* * *

Here is an evaluation exercise to help you become more aware of how well you are attending to the details of customer service. Read each of the following statements. For every one to which you can answer yes, you can feel good about your success. For every no, you'll see where you have room to grow your skills.

_____ Yes/No   Customers are greeted with eye contact, a smile, and a warm, genuine welcome when they arrive at your place of business.

_____ Yes/No   What the customer sees, hears, smells, feels, and possibly tastes at your place of business is pleasing and represents your company's values.

_____ Yes/No   You seek customer feedback to measure the quality of customers' interactions with your company.

_____ Yes/No   You have a system in place so that customers who must move from one service provider to another have a seamless transfer, and the next provider is up to speed on their situation.

_____ Yes/No   You ask your customers questions about their preferences, record those preferences, and use the information to make sure that they get the best possible service.

_____ Yes/No   You treat all your customers, regardless of the amount of business that they do with you, with the same respect and positive regard.

_____ Yes/No   You express appreciation to customers, coworkers, staff, and vendors on a daily basis.

_____ Yes/No When a customer is upset, you manage your emotions and offer support without defensiveness or frustration.

_____ Yes/No When a customer leaves your place of business or hangs up from a phone call, she feels good about her interaction with you.

GLADYS RESPONDS TO COMPASSION

"If you want others to be happy, practice compassion.
If you want to be happy, practice compassion."
—Dalai Lama

The Canfield Companies showed us that customer service is best provided when you take a compassionate, loving approach toward your customers. When you are kind, patient, and committed to their success, even your Gladys will fall in love with you, recommend you to others, and look forward to doing business with you again.

In Buddhist practice, there is a phrase,[1] "strong back, soft belly," that is used to describe how you sit during meditation: with a straight back and a relaxed stomach. It is also an excellent analogy for the best way to do business. You should have a "strong back," with processes and agreements in place that direct how you conduct business, coupled with a "soft belly" of openness and compassion for the people with whom you do business.

*   *   *

Over the next 30 days, run through this checklist each day and note your progress. Pay attention to which activities are easiest to apply and which take a bit more conscious effort. The more aware you become of compassionate behavior, the more yours will grow.

I. Grow Your Own Compassion—Every Day
_____ Be willing and eager to hear alternative points of view.
_____ Empathize by putting the customer's feelings into words, even when you disagree.

---

[1] _Brio Leadership_, "Developing Compassion & Courage: Strong Back, Soft Belly," blog posting on _www.brioleadership.com_, July 27, 2008.

_____ Listen more than you talk.

_____ Have an internal "no put-downs" rule.

_____ Verbalize your customers' and coworkers' wishes to make sure you understand them.

_____ Express appreciation every day.

_____ Answer repetitive questions graciously.

_____ Be fully present.

_____ Describe specifically what customers and coworkers are doing well.

_____ Talk about what your customers really want.

_____ Say no when you have to, without hostility.

_____ Show respect for your staff's readiness to learn new customer service skills.

_____ Model self-care to avoid burnout.

II. Grow Your Leadership Compassion—When a Service Provider Makes a Service Blunder:

_____ Express your feelings without attacking the employee's character.

_____ State your expectations.

_____ Offer a path to self-evaluation and self-correction.

_____ Offer choices.

_____ Encourage staff members to find the lesson learned in every mistake.

_____ Give staff members opportunities to attempt new skills.

_____ See mistakes as accelerated learning opportunities.

_____ Look for and acknowledge improvements.

_____ Be a storehouse for your staff's fine moments.

GLADYS RESPONDS TO PASSION

"Nothing great in the world has been accomplished without passion."
—Georg Wilhelm

The people at Paul Reed Smith Guitars bring passion to everything they do, from crafting beautiful instruments that are treasured by collectors and musicians to solving a customer's minor problem with a tuning peg or guitar case. When you are passionate about doing your best for customers, you will inevitably be a better service provider. Even your Gladys will respond to enthusiasm, and passion creates positive energy that draws customers to your business.

What if you were passionate about taking care of your customers? How can you develop your passion for service? What if you focused on what you love about your job?

There's a great saying that can alter your perspective: "If you don't have what you love, love what you have." Focus on what you enjoy and appreciate about your position, your company, and your product. This appreciation will help you fuel more passion for taking care of your customers. Soon you'll be feeling the pride that comes from satisfying customers beyond their expectations.

* * *

Here's an activity you can do to help you find passion in your job. Make a list of every aspect of customer service that is a regular part of your workday. For each aspect, fill in the following statement:

The thing I like most about _____ *is* _____.

Examples:

"The thing I like most about <u>serving customers</u> is <u>I like to help people</u>."
"The thing I like most about <u>dealing with complaints</u> is <u>I feel competent when I solve a problem</u>."

Get into the habit of looking for what you like about even the most challenging areas of customer service. You will find that your strengths and interests become clearer. Soon, you'll find that your focus has naturally moved toward what you like about your job, and your passion will spark.

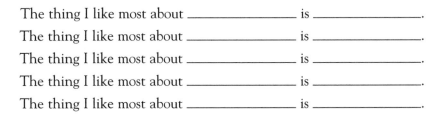

The thing I like most about _____ is _____.

The thing I like most about _____ is _____.

The thing I like most about _____ is _____.

The thing I like most about _____ is _____.

The thing I like most about _____ is _____.

GLADYS RESPONDS WHEN YOU GO THE EXTRA MILE

"There are no traffic jams when you go the extra mile."

—Anonymous

Singapore Airlines creates an emotional experience for its customers through its innovative practices. Since it would be easy for anyone to become a Gladys when she's confined to a plane for as much as 20 hours, the airline strives to exceed its customers' expectations and tend to the smallest details for their creature comforts. Its customers respond by booking the seats on Singapore flights to capacity. They don't mind paying a higher ticket price so that they can arrive at their destination feeling refreshed, even after 20 hours on a plane.

You can discover what aspects of your business are generating an emotional experience for your customers, both positive and negative, by listening closely to what they say and watching what they do. Pay attention to customers' responses. Design new services and product offerings based on your customers' needs and desires.

Have the courage to be innovative and take your service to higher levels. Ask staff members for their ideas for improving the customer experience. Ask "what if" questions and come up with small things that make a big difference.

* * *

How can you motivate yourself to go the extra mile? Be a "get-to" person, not a "have-to" person. Saying, "I get to calm an upset customer," creates a different mood from saying, "I have to calm an upset customer." Your mood affects your life and how inspired you are to put forth your best effort. It's often the simplest changes that have the most profound effects.

Instructions: For one week, catch yourself every time you say or think, "I have to." Notice how often the words show up. When they do, instead of beating yourself up, congratulate yourself. You cannot change what you do not notice. Shift your thinking and say to yourself, "I get to. . . ." With this simple shift in thinking, your inner resources will go to work for you, your mood will improve, and going the extra mile will become a more enjoyable, rewarding experience.

GLADYS RESPONDS WHEN YOU DON'T TAKE CONFLICT PERSONALLY

"Friendship is born at the moment when one person says to another: What! You, too? I thought I was the only one."
—C. S. Lewis

ISCO Corporation develops personal relationships with its customers, and this pays off in success. It also demonstrates how a personal commitment to providing the best possible service can practically eliminate competitive bids. When customers know that they can trust you, they are more confident and comfortable bringing you their business. And if something goes wrong, they're more forgiving.

What can you do to develop more personal relationships with your customers? Take a personal interest in their success. Build your personal reputation by acting with integrity so that your customers learn to trust you. Discover what you have in common so that conversation flows easily.

When your Gladys gets rattled, don't take it personally. Instead, take personal responsibility for setting things right. When you've developed a relationship with your customers, it's easier to make it through difficult times.

* * *

Make a personal commitment to implement what you've learned by taking a moment to write a plan for making a personal connection with your customers. Note the benefits that you, your customers, and your company will gain from putting your plan into action. Also, write down the possible consequences of not following through. Your growing awareness of the difference you can make will inspire you to make a positive change.

1. To grow my personal connection with my customers, I plan to:

   _____

   _____

   _____

   _____

2.   The benefits of carrying out my plan (to my customers, my company, and me) are:

_____

_____

_____

_____

3.   The consequences of not carrying out my plan (to my customers, my company, and me) would be:

_____

_____

_____

_____

GLADYS RESPONDS TO A LONG-TERM RELATIONSHIP

"It takes a long time to bring excellence to maturity."
—Publius Syrus

The Green Company showed us that patience is a virtue that can serve you and your company well. Its long-term approach to customer care has helped it earn high referral rates and weather difficult economic times. The company keeps in touch with its homeowners long after the sale is complete, even adding a department to help them with ongoing repairs and maintenance. As a result, its homeowners are happy, and the Green Company is one of the most well-respected builders and developers in its market.

Efforts to provide customer service must be consistent over extended time periods to show positive bottom-line results. Maintaining relationships with customers who have purchased from you is productive, since it generates referrals and repeat business that keep sales going during economic downturns. You can develop a longer-term focus by creating a system to keep in touch with customers. Make contact through e-mail, events, and scheduled calls every few months. The effort put into maintaining long-term relationships will pay off.

*   *   *

Customer Service Situation + Your Response
= Level of Customer Loyalty

You cannot always control the situation, but you always have a choice about how you respond to it. During your next staff meeting, list the ways you and your coworkers have responded to customer service situations that led to higher levels of customer loyalty. The more you build your awareness of what works well, the more it becomes a natural part of how you do business. Adding activities like this one to your regular meetings will create more consistent use of the best customer service practices.

Customer Service Situation + Your Response
= Level of Customer Loyalty

Customer service situation:

_____

_____

Your response:

_____

_____

Level of customer loyalty: higher/same/lower

Encourage each other to write winning formulas of your own, like:

Unhappy Customer + My Better-than-Expected Response = Delighted Customer

Satisfied Customer + My Ongoing Support = My Business Is Fondly Remembered

GLADYS RESPONDS TO A WELL-TRAINED STAFF

"Players win games. Teams win championships."
—Bill Taylor

Preston Wynne Spa has a dedicated team that is enthusiastic about serving its customers. When the spa needs to hire someone, it looks for people with healthy self-esteem and a positive attitude. It is slow to hire and quick to fire, knowing that people who don't contribute to the positive environment should be encouraged to find more suitable employment somewhere else. It also realizes the importance of ongoing training and communication to keep its staff informed and motivated. A well-trained staff is better prepared to manage any Gladys it might encounter.

How can you strengthen your team so that it's able to deliver the best possible customer service? Constant communication supports excellent service. Create internal "contests" to encourage service excellence. Offer employees feedback tools to handle complaints and recurring issues effectively. Make sure employees know that when they're complaining without a focus on solutions, they're contributing to the problem. A productive complaint requires action on the part of the employee so that the problem gets solved.

* * *

A high intention to make your customers happy can take your company far. However, along with high intentions, the members of your team may have high attachments to their own way of doing things or to their own specific ideas about how to make customers happy. They may become emotionally attached to their ideas, resisting change or opposing thoughts.

Teamwork breaks down fast when people have high attachments. To have a high intention with low attachment means that you hold fast to the overall goal, letting go of the emotional need to see your way as the only way. High attachment can lead to heated arguments and disconnected team members. When you have a low attachment, you are open-minded, so it is easier for you to allow something even better to happen. Mention this concept to a group of people, and in all likelihood, they will reassure you that "high intention/low attachment" is easy for them. Here is an exercise to help reinforce the concept in an emotion-affecting way:

1. Purchase a set of engraved or inked rocks, wood plaques, metal keychains, pens, or other gift items, each having an inspirational word on it—words like Success, Passion, Wisdom, Vitality, Wealth, Peace, Cooperation, Fun, and Freedom.

2. Place the items in a basket and have each team member pull one out.

3. Ask each team member to look at her word and imagine how that word can enrich or assist her in her life. Give all the team members time to think about it.

4. Next, ask each team member to give her item away to another team member, so that everyone ends up with a new word.

5. Ask the question: "Did you feel a bit of resistance giving up the one you originally picked?" People are surprised by the emotional attachment they make so quickly to even something small that they consider "theirs." Many are also surprised by how delightful it feels to receive their new word, something that they may consider better than what they had.

6. Debrief with the group. Have a discussion about how each person at one time or another will have a point of view to which he is so attached that it may be difficult to consider other viewpoints.

7. Place the phrase "High Intention/Low Attachment" in your meeting room as a reminder.

GLADYS RESPONDS TO TWO-WAY COMMUNICATION

"A good listener is not only popular everywhere,
but after a while, he gets to know something."

—Wilson Mizner

ClearVision Optical has climbed to the top ranks of customer service in its industry using two-way communication. It seeks customer and employee input—both negative and positive—through surveys, meetings, and events. It acts on the information it discovers, improving its operations and products based on the feedback it receives. For an added personal touch and to keep management connected with every Gladys, any customer that complains gets a personal call from the company president.

How can you enhance the two-way communication at your place of business? Seek customer and employee input through surveys, meetings, telephone calls, and events. Act on the information you find out. Put customer and employee ideas about how to improve your product or service into action. View negative feedback as an opportunity to improve your processes.

Two-way communication also means making sure that your staff and clients know what they need to know. Convey information to customers regularly with a colorful and engaging newsletter or e-mail piece. Make it easy for your clients to understand your policies and procedures. Clearly spell out standard processes for your staff, and then review them and how they are being followed. Show appreciation to employees for their good work and the good feelings you generate will flow through to the customer. Take good care of your employees and they will take good care of your clients.

* * *

Consider how often you feel stressed when you receive negative feedback. When you view challenges as problems, you can become less resilient and may feel less inclined to seek opinions in the future. Seeing the gift in what you might consider "bad news" will raise your ability to deliver the best possible customer service. You might wonder, "Where is the gift in having a hysterical customer yell at me when an order didn't arrive on time?" The gifts are many, including these: (1) you get the opportunity to investigate the processes that led to your product showing up late, so that it won't happen again; (2) you get a chance to grow your emotion management skills, so that you can remain present and resourceful; and (3) if you totally lose your cool, you get to look for the lesson and seek out ways to do better next time.

In the left-hand column, briefly describe three of the most recent customer service situations that you viewed as "bad." Then, in the right-hand column, write down a gift that each of those bad situations gave you.

Bad Customer Service Situation:	Gift I Received from This Situation:
1. _____	_____
2. _____	_____
3. _____	_____

GLADYS RESPONDS TO CONTINUOUS IMPROVEMENT

*"There's always room for improvement, you know.
It's the biggest room in the house."*

—Louise Heath Leber

Sky Lakes Medical Center is committed to continually improving its customer service. It uses everything from basic guidelines, like the "six-foot rule" that requires employees to greet anyone who is within six feet of them, to more expansive initiatives that require workshops and performance improvement teams. High-performing employees are appointed to train their peers and serve as leaders for process improvement efforts.

The management team at Sky Lakes honors every employee for the part she plays in the patient's overall experience. It gives staff members the authority to determine when more than just an apology is required to make things right after a mistake or misunderstanding. It is widely acknowledged that everyone at Sky Lakes has contributed to the hospital's improved customer service scores. As a result, employees are fully on board and committed to doing what it takes to improve the quality of customer service. After all, having exceptional customer service means that your Gladys will be at her best, too.

You get what you measure. Bring continuous improvement to your company by measuring your customer satisfaction with surveys and other tools. Make advancing overall quality a part of every employee's job description. Engage all the managers in the effort, and hold them accountable for quality within their area of the business. Acknowledge enthusiastic staff members for their efforts, and engage them in training their peers. Before you know it, your customer service could render your competition virtually irrelevant.

* * *

Here is a brainstorming activity that can help you come up with steps to improve customer service at your place of business. Either with your team or on your own, complete the following statements.

If I were to put 5 percent more effort into my customer service efforts, I would

_____.

If I were to spend 5 percent more time improving processes, I would

_____.

If I were 5 percent more excited about creating a happier work environment, I would

_____.

If I were 5 percent less afraid to take a risk, I would suggest that we

_____.

If I were to listen 5 percent more to what customers say, I would

_____.

If I were to offer 5 percent more team effort, I would

_____.

GLADYS RESPONDS TO CREATIVE PROBLEM SOLVING

"Whatever creativity is, it is, in part, a solution to a problem."
                                                    —Brian Aldiss

The Communicore team knows that creative problem solving means going beyond the first solution to the best solution. When one of the firm's staff members discovers a problem or error, he informs the customer immediately and sets about solving it. Employees know that how they manage a problem can actually strengthen the client relationship. They go out of their way to solve issues that come up, even if it means sacrificing their personal time on nights and weekends to meet client deadlines.

What would happen if you implemented a "three-solution rule" for every problematic issue that arises? If you've "hit the wall" and can't come up with a solution, bring in an outsider who may bring a fresh perspective and the answer. When you discover a problem, develop a process that puts an end to it so that other customers don't have to contend with the same issue. Take personal responsibility for making sure that the new process is implemented.

Be willing to do the heavy lifting in the customer relationship, and put in the extra emotional effort to thaw out a chilly Gladys. It often pays off. Learn to distinguish when a prospect will not be a proper fit to do business with your company, watching for the red flags of customers who will create too high a toll on your staff. Fine-tune your instincts to sense when a customer's lack of integrity and refusal to follow procedures make it unwise to continue a business relationship. Watch for the red flags from those who will require major effort for little or no reward.

* * *

Here's an unlikely activity to help you become more creative: Stop thinking. Consider a customer service problem that you are currently struggling with, and then stop thinking. Sit quietly. Focus on your breath and put yourself in a state of relaxation. When you're feeling stuck, the fastest way to get your creative juices flowing again is to create a space of internal silence. If you have five minutes to spare, try it right now. Sit quietly. Close your eyes and silence your mind. In less than a minute, once your thoughts have quieted, inspired ideas will start coming to you. Don't think about them; just let them come to the surface of your awareness. It helps to have a pencil and paper nearby to jot them down as they come to you. This process is similar to rebooting a computer. It restarts your creativity and gets you back on track when you're feeling stopped.

The Practical Points

The following list can serve as a reminder of what you can do right now to improve your customer service skills. You can download this list as a PDF file at www.WhosYourGladys.com/PracticalPoints.

- Be fully present.
- Value and learn from your mistakes.
- Empathize with your customers.
- Pick a role model with the qualities you want to develop.
- Meet unique customer needs.
- Establish trust.
- Answer repetitive questions graciously.
- See customers as people, not as problems.
- Make decisions that delight customers.
- Do what you love to do.
- Seek to know what your customers know.
- Act in alignment with your company's brand.
- Do what you say you're going to do.
- Think and act like a champion.
- Anticipate customer preferences.
- Give customers some control over their experience.
- Seek out emotional responses.
- Communicate a message of innovation and hospitality.
- Cater to customers' lifestyles.
- Strive to exceed expectations.
- Deliver credible interactions.
- See the positive quality of a client's negative behavior.
- Feel compassion while your customers vent their emotions.
- Get to know and care about your customers.

- Give your customers what they need.
- Put care into the details of your everyday actions.
- View challenging situations as opportunities to make the client relationship even stronger.
- Honor the customs of your customers.
- Use long-term thinking.
- Develop win-win relationships.
- Think like an entrepreneur, regardless of your job description.
- Put your customers first.
- Be a creative problem solver.
- Treat customers the way *they* want to be treated.
- Ask useful questions.
- Offer low pressure and high pleasure.
- Focus on the benefits.
- Manage the customers' expectations.
- Consider your customers' perceptions.
- Do the right thing.
- Offer continuous points of contact.
- Maintain the relationship during and after the sale.
- Create an excellent first impression.
- Put the right people on the job.
- Respond positively to a variety of communication styles.
- Contribute to a happy work environment.
- Present a consistent artistic service performance.
- Evaluate results and make improvements.
- Make sure all customer interactions end on a happy note.
- Gain a competitive advantage by giving strong customer service.
- Use surveys to gain valuable information about what customers want.
- Respond to a customer's complaints through personal contact.
- Be fair, even when you think the customer is wrong.
- Use a wide variety of feedback tools.
- Communicate your customer service philosophy with employees regularly.
- Give and receive ongoing training.
- Cultivate a culture of inclusivity.
- See every complaint as a gift.
- Educate and empower front-line staff.
- Implement customer service best practices continuously.

> Use service recovery tools.
> Appreciate employees for what they're doing right.
> Be nice.
> Be honest.
> Take complete responsibility for a speedy recovery.
> Strengthen the relationship with every interaction.
> Use both your heart and your head.
> Take action when you discover a problem.
> Find joy in turning around negative customer interactions.
> Know when to say good-bye.

Recommended "Who's Your Gladys?" Resources

PROGRAMS TO HELP YOU PUT THE 10 PRINCIPLES OF THIS BOOK TO IMMEDIATE USE

Now that you have the tools for successfully managing your Gladys and all of your client relationships, you may want to set your sights on creating more customer service success in your business. The sooner you put these tools into practice, the better the results you'll enjoy with your customers. To assist you in speeding up your progress, we created the following programs to provide greater support than you can get from a book alone.

"Who's Your Gladys?" Workshops

In the workshop, you will be personally guided in applying these principles, tools, and habits to get immediate results and build upon a solid foundation. You will put the cornerstones of quality customer service into practice. You'll gain emotion management skills and learn to apply a creative approach to problem solving.

"Who's Your Gladys?" Coaching

Even the most skilled professionals run into challenges and need some personal guidance. The best professionals are known to enlist ongoing coaching to continuously build forward momentum so that they can accomplish more. Coaching will aid your development and help you to think, feel, and act in ways that support your dreams and transform your workplace results.

"Who's Your Gladys?" Interview Series

Marilyn Suttle and Lori Jo Vest offer in-depth interviews with the most exquisite customer service providers, from CEOs to front-line staff. Learning how they think, feel, and act will allow you to bring profound positive change to your business. Gain inspiration and a clear vision of the many ways you can turn every customer, including your Gladys, into a loyal fan.

"Who's Your Gladys?" Keynote Presentation

With more than 15 years' experience giving keynote presentations for corporations and associations, Marilyn Suttle has transformed the thinking and inspired action in corporate and association audiences through emotional connection, usable tools, and humor. Bring your people together to educate them, entertain them, and ignite a desire in them to create meaningful, heartfelt, humanizing connections with customers, coworkers, and colleagues.

For more information on these and other programs available, please visit www.WhosYourGladys.com.

PERSONAL AND PROFESSIONAL GROWTH TOOLS AND TECHNIQUES

The Canfield Group—Jack Canfield, CSP, CPAE

www.JackCanfield.com

The Canfield Group offers life-changing programs that focus on living the success principles, raising self-esteem, and optimizing peak performance. Jack Canfield, known as America's #1 Success Coach, helps you get from where you are to where you want to be.

Family Constellation—Jo Erickson

www.TheLifeLearningCenter.net

The Family Constellation is group work that is used to release profound tensions within and between people. Those tensions may lie in a personal or professional context. It helps resolve misunderstandings, entanglements, and blocks in the attendees' families, with partners, and in professional relationships.

The Hoffman Institute Foundation

www.HoffmanInstitute.org

The Hoffman Process is a powerful experience involving the reeducation of love. During the eight-day residential process, students learn to integrate the four aspects of self—physical, intellectual, emotional, and spiritual—by untying the emotional knots that link us to negative patterns learned as children. Once the layers of negative patterns are peeled away, one can discover intrinsic authenticity, compassion, creativity, lovability, and a sense of joy!

Humanity Unites Brilliance

www.hubhub.org

Humanity Unites Brilliance is a uniting place for people and organizations to come together and move the world from survival, to self-sustainability, to self-empowerment. It offers a new model for business and humanitarian living, a social community supported by a powerful social marketing program, a source where you can gain access to the finest tools, and resources and products to help you use your passions to transform yourself and the world—including the world's most inspirational educators, bestselling empowerment authors, top empowerment curricula, and more.

Inscape Profiles/Assessments/Instruments

www.inscapepublishing.com

Inscape Publishing is the world's leading provider of DiSC-based classroom learning solutions. Its training products develop critical interpersonal business skills such as sales, leadership, management, team building, and communication.

Option Method—Lenora Boyle

www.ChangeLimitingBeliefs.com

Lenora Boyle has been helping people to be happier since 1991 through her interactive seminars, private coaching practice, and teleclasses. She teaches seminars using the Option Method, which specializes in going to the root of the problem: the limiting belief or past conditioning.

Ludi-Q's—Jan Black

www.ludiqs.com

This provides priceless clarity at the speed of a flip. Ludi-Q's are shortcuts to clarity that quickly train you to read the unspoken ludicrous questions that confuse, frustrate, and sabotage you, your relationships, your career, and/or your business.

ShawneTV—Shawne Duperon

www.ShawneTV.com

Five-time Emmy® Award-winning producer Shawne Duperon has taught thousands all across North America how to get free publicity and increase business. This Media & Gossip (word-of-mouth) expert has been seen on major networks and featured in *USA Today*, the *Wall Street Journal*, and the *Chicago Tribune*, to name only a few publications.

Releasing the Inner Magician (RIM)—Dr. Deborah Sandella

www.InnerMagician.com

The RIM method is an advanced mind-body method for releasing the past and rewiring sabotaging thoughts and feelings. RIM helps you tap your inner magician—the divine intuitive power within that dissolves pain to reveal the natural strength and passion of your spirit.

Keynote Concerts—Jana Stanfield, CSP, Queen of Heavy Mental

Motivational Music, www.JanaStanfield.com

Jana is a keynote speaker at conferences and corporate events. Her songs educate, energize, and inspire. Jana describes her music as "psychotherapy you can dance to."

BUSINESS TRAINING

Custom Learning Systems—Brian Lee, CSP
HealthCare Service Excellence Institute

www.CustomLearning.com

Using proven methods, the CLS team improves patient and resident satisfaction and implements a dynamic culture change process to sustain results. It is the leader in on-site training, coaching, and service education in the health-care industry. E-mail: brian@customlearning.com.

Morgan Seminar Group—Rebecca Morgan, CSP, CMC

www.RebeccaMorgan.com

Rebecca Morgan is an internationally sought-after management consultant and presenter, and a best-selling author on developing your key talent.

Thank You Very Much, Inc.—Holly Stiel, CSP

www.ThankYouVeryMuchInc.com

After 17 years as a concierge, Holly Stiel started Thank You Very Much, Inc., to adapt hotel concierge service levels and philosophy to all kinds of businesses.

Brio Leadership, Inc.—Kristin Roberts, Founder

www.BrioLeadership.com

Brio Leadership helps individuals and teams incorporate spiritual intelligence into their workplaces and live lives of integrity, meaning, and fulfillment. Incorporating spiritual intelligence into the workplace is a call to bring our highest selves to work every day.

CUSTOMER COMMUNICATION TOOLS

SurveyMonkey

www.SurveyMonkey.com

SurveyMonkey enables anyone to create professional online surveys quickly and easily.

Avidian Prophet Software

www.avidian.com

Prophet provides a contact management solution that works within your Outlook contact database. It allows you to send group e-mails and manage customer activity records easily and efficiently.

PROFESSIONAL AND PERSONAL DEVELOPMENT BOOKS

10 Secrets for Success and Inner Peace, Dr. Wayne Dyer (Carlsbad, CA: Hay House, 2001).

Ask and It Is Given: Learning to Manifest Your Desires, Jerry and Esther Hicks (Carlsbad, CA: Hay House, 2005).

Blink: The Power of Thinking Without Thinking, Malcolm Gladwell (New York: Little, Brown & Company, 2005).

Calming Upset Customers: Staying Effective During Unpleasant Situations, Rebecca Morgan (Ontario, Canada: Crisp Learning, 2002).

Care Packages for Your Customers, Barbara Glanz (New York: McGraw-Hill, 2007).

Delivering Knock Your Socks Off Service, Performance Research Associates (New York: AMACOM, 2006).

Emotional Value: Creating Strong Bonds with Your Customers, Janelle Barlow and Dianna Maul (San Francisco: Berrett-Koehler Publishers, Inc., 2000).

The Global Consultant: How to Make Seven Figures Across Borders, Alan Weiss and Omar Khan (Hoboken, NJ: Wiley, 2008).

Good to Great: Why Some Companies Make the Leap . . . and Others Don't, Jim Collins (New York: HarperCollins, 2001).

Happy for No Reason: Seven Steps to Being Happy from the Inside Out, Marci Shimoff (New York: Free Press, 2008).

Learned Optimism: How to Change Your Mind and Your Life, Martin Seligman (New York: Vintage, 2006).

Loving What Is: Four Questions That Can Change Your Life, Byron Katie (New York: Three Rivers Press, 2003).

Neon Signs of Service: Getting to the Heart of the Matter in Customer Service, Holly Stiel (Tucson: AZ Press, 2002).

Nonviolent Communication: A Language of Life, Marshall B. Rosenberg (Encinitas, CA: PuddleDancer Press, 2003).

The Nordstrom Way to Customer Service Excellence: A Handbook for Implementing Great Service in Your Organization, Robert Spector (Hoboken, NJ: Wiley, 2005).

One Small Step Can Change Your Life: The Kaizen Way, Robert Maurer, Ph.D. (New York: Workman Publishing Company, 2004).

Overcoming Underearning: Overcome Your Money Fears and Earn What You Deserve, Barbara Stanny (New York: HarperCollins, 2005).

Satisfaction Guaranteed: How to Satisfy Every Customer Every Time!, Brian Lee (Alberta, Canada: Mastery Publishing, 1996).

Saying Yes to Life: Even the Hard Parts, Ezra Bayda with Josh Bartok (Somerville, MA: Wisdom Publications, 2005).

The Sedona Method: Your Key to Lasting Happiness, Success, Peace and Emotional Well-Being, Hale Dwoskin (Sedona, AZ: Sedona Press, 2003).

Small Giants: Companies That Choose to Be Great Instead of Big, Bo Burlingham (New York: Penguin Group, 2005).

StrengthsFinder 2.0: A New and Upgraded Edition of the Online Test from Gallup's Now Discover Your Strengths, Tom Rath (New York: Gallup Press, 2007).

Success Built to Last: Creating a Life That Matters, Jerry Porras, Stewart Emery, and Mark Thompson (New York: Plume, 2007).

The Success Principles: How to Get from Where You Are to Where You Want to Be, Jack Canfield (New York: HarperCollins, 2005).

Whale Done!: The Power of Positive Relationships, Kenneth Blanchard, Thad Lacinak, Chuck Tompkins, and Jim Ballard (New York: Free Press, 2002).

Why You're Dumb, Sick & Broke . . . And How to Get Smart, Healthy & Rich!, Randy Gage (Hoboken, NJ: Wiley, 2006).

Zingerman's Guide to Giving Great Service: Treating Your Customers Like Royalty, Ari Weinzweig (New York: Hyperion Books, 2003).

Index